ON THE ROAD

I dedicate this book to all the people
over the centuries who have walked the camino.
Without their inspiration,
taking the journey
would never have occurred to us.

TO John, my devoted editor who, with surprising
patience has jogged my memory and stimulated
both composition and structure.

TO my three intrepid daughters who made our
passage over road and tracks a delight.

TO supporting friends, Josephine Bastian,
Anna Leacock and Sarah Stackman,
who guided me at
critical moments.

ON THE ROAD

A FAMILY TREKKING TO COMPOSTELLA IN 1973

Hilary James

Svengali Press and ETT Imprint
2017

On the Road: A family trekking to Compostella in 1973

First published by West Grinstead Publishers 2015
Second Edition published in e-book and Print-on-Demand (POD) format
    by The Svengali Press & ETT Imprint 2017
© Hilary James 2015, 2017
Photography by Hilary James
ISBN: 978-1-925416-72-5 (ebook)
ISBN: 978-1-925416-73-2 (paper)

&
The Svengali Press

PO Box 1852
Strawberry Hills
NSW 2012
AUSTRALIA
http://www.svengalipress.com.au

ETT Imprint
PO Box R1906
Royal Exchange
NSW 1225
AUSTRALIA

TABLE OF CONTENTS

1

PREPARING FOR A PILGRIMAGE

From this day forth
I shall be called a wanderer
　　Basho -17th century Japanese poet and pilgrim

"What are we going to take with us?" Rebecca's pack had nothing inside it yet.

"Not much," I said. "We will be walking for weeks so you won't want to carry more than you have to."

The girls appreciated that thought.

For this would be the biggest walk of our lives, from Chartres in northern France to Santiago de Compostella in north-west Spain. And today we were actually packing.

We were sitting on the floor of our tiny cedar cottage, Red Pomme, our clothes spread around us. As long-term travellers we had few to choose from, but we were enjoying the process.

Though we would not be taking much, medieval pilgrims would have taken far less. No more than could have been fitted into one of their scrips, a small deerskin satchel.

After putting in our jeans and shirts, a jumper, underwear and a wind-jacket, our clothes were packed by the time John came home from the cathedral. He was an architectural historian and had been studying Chartres Cathedral in detail for the last few years. Now he was finding it hard to let go.

"We are ready," Emily said as he came in. "What are you going to take, Dad?"

"Not much, I guess," he said.

Pilgrims taking the camino today often start with packs that are far too heavy, and find they have to reluctantly post things home to handle the weight. Back then we did not have that problem, as inveterate travellers being Spartan was our motto.

John and I were more concerned with what we could not take, like sleeping bags. They would be too bulky and heavy for the girls to carry. But how would we manage without them? We expected to stay in youth hostels as usual where we would need our sleeping sheets. But what about times when we did not find a hostel? It was already October and starting to get chilly.

Out of faith or innocence, John shrugged it off with "We will manage somehow."

Books went into our luggage of course. No one questioned that. When one of my friends recently walked to Compostela she chose not to take any and said she was glad of it, but we couldn't imagine that.

Organ Morgan parked next to Red Pomme where we planned this journey

There was still some hesitation around a heavy bulky paperback copy of Tolstoy's *War and Peace*. This had been John's Christmas present that we had been reading aloud to the family, for we had watched it on a BBC programme in Scotland. Television had been a rare experience in our lives, so its impact had been very strong. No-one wanted to leave it behind.

"We could make it lighter. What if we ripped off the section we have read and then tore off each chapter as we finished it?" John suggested.

I was shocked. I wouldn't do that to a book. But the girls liked the idea, so I gave in. It could be a game.

Books were closely part of our lives. Emily recently told me, "Always in Europe we yearned to find more books in English as we did not take many with us. There was wild abandon whenever we came across any."

Cassandra asked, "What did medieval pilgrims take with them?"

"Cloaks and broad hats and staves," I listed. "And I don't know what else. Do you, John?"

"They wore sandals on their feet and carried a shell if they were going to Santiago. It was a symbol that marked them off from pilgrims going to Jerusalem who carried a palm leaf."

On this trip John was walking in sand-shoes. The girls and I preferred open sandals since they were easy to slip out of when we wanted to walk barefoot.

Cassandra already had her staff. In the previous winter in Italy she had cut a branch from an olive tree in the mountains. Peeling off the bark and oiling it well she made herself a walking stick, though she had no idea a pilgrimage was ahead. Now Rebecca and Emily took up her idea, hurrying into the woods to find their own pilgrim staffs. In rougher medieval times a staff was useful as a protection against attack and a help in crossing turbulent streams.

Emily added a distinctive touch to hers by putting one of her red snow mittens on the top. This had begun as a gesture of the moment but remained a permanent talisman.

Rebecca at twelve and a half was as tall as Cassandra, who was fourteen. She almost looked like her twin. Emily had just turned ten and was noticeably smaller and younger than the others

Rebecca had stitched onto the back of her pack a magnificent golden butterfly. Her other personal addition to her luggage was a water bottle that dangled from the back. None of us thought of this, for carrying drinking water had not yet become the fashion it is today.

Cassandra wanted to bring the purple tweed cloak she had embroidered the year before in Scotland. She had been copying the Viking style as she loved to read about those turbulent times. But a wind jacket seemed more practical than a long cloak, so her gown was sadly packed away in a friend's cellar.

We did not think of hats against the sun, but the girls were going to wear their traditional Balinese headbands that they had bought there two years earlier.

Rebecca and Cassandra also carried useful pocketknives attached to their belts. I don't remember how their interest in knives had started, though I had done the same as a girl.

Cockleshells would complete our outfit and we could see them in the window of an elegant charcuterie in town. They were filled with a mouth-watering fish concoction in a white wine sauce. The dish was sold under the enticing name of Coquilles Saint Jacques, the patron saint of Santiago. But five shells were too dear to think of.

Pilgrims originally picked up their cockleshells on the beach in Galicia or from the fishermen, collecting them as they went. They were useful not just as a symbol, but as spoons to dip into communal stews in monasteries, or a way of scooping up water. But we would have to do without.

There was much uncertainty in our planning, for in 1973 there were few pilgrims walking to Santiago de Compostella and no books of experiences to draw from. But ever since the 1980's the pilgrimage has become increasingly popular, and advice is easy to come upon. From his studies John knew there was a wide choice of roads to choose from.

For centuries pilgrims have poured into Spain from every part of Europe including Italy or through southern Spain and even by ship from England or Scandinavia. There was a passion to visit the burial place of this early saint. But since the twelfth century the most popular one has been the French Way through Roncevalles across the mountains.

It was a dangerous journey. As churchmen found pilgrim numbers increasing, they realised that protection and assistance would be needed. So they started providing beds and food and security for them in the Clunaic monasteries. The first European travel guide was written at that time. It followed the French Way and publicized

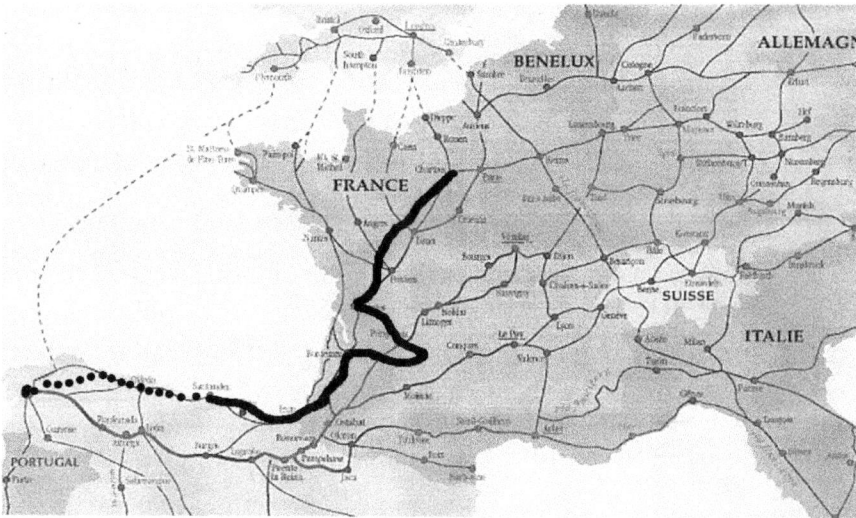

Rebecca: *A myriad of well-beaten tracks converge on Compostella like a fishing net drawing in the faithful. As an agnostic teenager I was surprised that the Way had its influence on me. In the focussed solitude of a long walk I had time to explore my own thoughts in a new way.*

it even further. Pilgrims today most commonly choose this same path into Spain.

We decided not to go over the steep Pyrenees, but to follow another old route, south through France to San Sebastian then west along the pleasant Spanish coast to Santiago. The Spanish section of this was called the English Way as their pilgrims often began the journey by boat.

"I haven't told you," John said at the end of our talk. "I met Pére Robert in the cathedral. He has given me the letter he promised for our pilgrimage."

When John had told the curé of Chartres cathedral that we were going on the camino he had generously offered to write us a letter of introduction for the priests and nuns we met along our way:

M and Mme James and their three daughters are going by foot on the pilgrimage to Santiago de Compostella. M James has worked regularly for four years in Chartres on a very powerful architectural study of the cathedral. His pilgrimage is in line with his research. I would be appreciative if you can support them.

His letter made clear that our pilgrimage was not a religious one: He knew we were spiritual seekers in a different way, more like most pilgrims today. We have found that the Catholic church makes everyone welcome; one's intention is all that matters.

Eagerly we looked over the letter and knew it would be a blessing. It turned out to be tremendously

important as it gave us choice of accommodation, and much more. It was to provide the key that unlocked doors to resting places and relationships with people we would otherwise have never known.

Father Robert had come to know us well. We had been living in Europe for four years and spent three months each year in Chartres to allow for John's passionate research of the cathedral. Over that time the old building had become part of our daily lives.

We used the cathedral as another home. We were free to wander there in those easy times, for John had been given access to the whole building through being gifted a huge, decorative clanking set of keys. At that time, unlike today, security was very relaxed.

After shopping at the Saturday market we would stow our goods on the bottom steps of the cold limestone staircase, before going up top, stepping past nesting pigeons.

To enter the main west front of the cathedral you pushed hard on its heavy swinging leather studded doors. They formed a barrier between the modern world outside and the dark spiritual interior where you found yourself in semi-darkness standing on a cold-smelling stone floor. So your eyes were naturally drawn upwards to the light. High above glorious medieval stained glass windows poured down an intensity of colour, blues, dark reds, purples and yellows.

In one way or another we dropped in there every day.

We would picnic on the rooftop with the town spread out below. When friends called we took them up to this private place and shared a great experience. Though we were not of any religion, the essence of the cathedral subtly soaked through us all.

This was the background to our camino, so that it felt natural to take up John's suggestion and go on a pilgrimage to the burial place of an unknown saint in the distant corner of western Spain. We knew that whatever happened it would be enriching.

2

THE FIRST DAY

*We were told the history of the walk before we left. It became
the background to our imaginative games. We bought sturdy sandals
and the shared items were carefully apportioned. I carried the
Vegemite and cutlery, a very poor effort my sisters felt.*
  Emily

We had planned to set out on our pilgrimage in summer, but weeks
kept slipping by with John still clambering over the cathedral, tape
in one hand and camera round his neck, while he untangled further
complexities of its building history.

We were growing increasingly restless, disappointed at being
held back for so long. As flocks of swallows flew past on their
migratory path we yearned to be on our way too. Would he ever feel
he had completed his work?

But I also knew this was his last opportunity to work on site
before we returned to Australia.

Then just when we were really losing heart, he said he was
finished and it was time to go.

It was the ninth of October and we left from Saumur, a little town in the wine-growing district of the Loire. It would have been more significant to have left from the great western doors of Chartres cathedral: how right to have been waved off by the sculptured kings and queens of the Royal Portal. But that would have forced us to walk through suburbs along a busy modern highway and over the endless flat wheat-fields of the Beauce.

Instead, we began with a leisurely home lunch with our friends Dominique and Poupette. Their main question about our trip was the same as that of all our French friends. "How will you manage three meals each day?" That seemed a very French concern, and we just brushed it aside.

Dominique drove us to Chartres station where we caught a small train south. It connected with a leisurely bus that dropped us at the end of the afternoon outside the youth hostel at Saumur.

A big group of German schoolboys and their teachers were installed there, but there were still ample empty beds for us.

After dinner everyone crowded round the living-room fire, chairs squeezed close alongside sofas. Young energy filled the room. Led by a teacher's guitar we sang folk songs in two languages.

When we left in the morning the German kids were already in their bus. "Goodbye," they called to us in English and "Auf Wiedersehen" we replied, proud to have a word or two of German. They were going back to their home town in the north while we were heading boldly in the opposite direction.

We walked out of town briskly, sniffing the tangy freshness of the air and aware of the new feeling of our packs settling on our backs. At last, at last, we were pilgrims.

Cassandra: *John's mapped plan for us to walk south through the quiet backroads and paths, a letter of introduction asking the church to help us on our way, our staffs, sandals, and legs we thought were fit - it felt it was going to be amazing!*

We had wondered if we were setting off too late; but on this day the weather was perfect. Wild-flowers bloomed thick along the

road-side and birds were singing with abandon, whirling through the air so close to us that we could hear the buzz of their wings. Everything around us was rejoicing with us. We sang as we walked and felt at one with nature.

Along the roadside we saw many vineyards. The grape pickers wore large wicker conical baskets on their backs and tossed the grapes into them over their shoulders. They were having the biggest harvest for years. Vignerons kept calling to us as we passed, "Come and pick grapes with us."

We were actually being offered jobs, the whole family, no experience needed. It was very tempting.

When this first happened we were astounded and proud. But it happened again and again over the following days so we grew blasé; though we were impressed when one man was so eager to have us that he chased after us on his bicycle.

These tempting offers had come too soon. We had not yet had time to start being pilgrims. So we waved them aside with thanks and kept walking, nibbling bunches of grapes. And yet it left us with a hankering for something missed. What if we had paused on that first day? What extra experiences would we have had?

Autumn's fecundity lay all around. The apple and walnut trees along the roadside were also laden and we filled our pockets with nuts.

"We are nut-grazers," we said, cracking them open with stones. We added to this feast sweet blackberries from the woods. Their prickles made collecting difficult, but the flavour would be all the more satisfying after a scrambling struggle. You become a hunter rather than a gatherer as you reach high for the sprays that avoid you.

We thought of Basho, the pilgrim poet. His long spiritual

walking trips in wild seventeenth century Japan took him down
roads similar to those of our medieval pilgrims. Like us he found
fruits to feast on like tasty wild plums half hidden in the thickets.

We came to a cross road and stopped to look at our map. John
found a place to spread it out while we crowded round curiously,
tracing its tracks and roads with our fingers.

"Here is a list of the symbols the French Michelin maps use," John said. "Once you can recognise them the map makes sense. These maps show all grades of roads, even foot paths. Here's one going through a forest. These are the large-scale maps we are going to follow. We will mostly keep on simple fourth- class roads. That way we will avoid the traffic." Not that there many cars on these quiet back-roads, and they were usually local.

I was glad John had a natural sense of direction for I had none. On my own I would have drifted happily from place to place, ending up anywhere.

By following John's plan, we would be walking steadily, day after day, week after week, over the map as our fingers were doing now until we came to Spain. We would finally arrive at Santiago close to the Portuguese border and the Atlantic Ocean.

"How far away is this place?" asked Rebecca. "I know this is a local map, but how does it join up with the whole of the trip?"

John brought out our large map and showed us the full extent of our journey. Until this moment I had not grasped its immensity. It seemed it was going to go on forever. And would I have the stamina for it? I knew John would, but my stamina would be supported by my optimism, not by any real knowledge of what my body would be capable of doing. Would the girls really be able to keep up with it? At that moment with such hugeness in front of me my positiveness slipped away, leaving me uncertain for us all. I was feeling rather serious as we folded up the maps.

"Who is Saint James and why was he so special that pilgrims have trekked down there for all these centuries?" Cassandra asked.

That led John to describe the myth that has become woven around one of Jesus' disciples whose body was said to have travelled from Jerusalem and turned up in Santiago in a stone boat.

The myths that gathered around him did not swell to their fullness until the ninth century, and as they fitted in with the political needs of those times they grew stronger with time.

Following the path John had showed us on the map, we left the vineyards and were walking through a forest. By the middle of the day it was time for our lunch break.

We pulled out a long French loaf, a cheese and pate and fruit, and also our favourite drink, Jus de Pomme, picked up in the last village.

French apple juice was such a favourite with the girls that Emily had decided she would name a child of hers Jus-de-Pomme. "It will be a perfect name for a boy," she said with certainty.

After our picnic we spread out comfortably on carpets of leaves and took turns to read aloud from *War and Peace*. From its first words, the book's canvas prepared us to be stretched wide.

The story started with a grand party in Moscow held at a time when the world was poised between the innocence and complacency of peace and the threat of war with Napoleon. We were introduced to a big group of Russian upper class people, and listened to their flirting and scheming. Most of the major characters in this vast book were introduced on this occasion. Later we would follow them through the ravages of the long war that followed.

At this party a diffident young man, Pierre, had just come home from being educated in Paris. He was ill at ease in society and got brushed aside by the worldly. All the more so because he was illegitimate and had no status or money.

But his life was about to change. We were excited to closely follow his story and those of his friends, the charming innocent Bolkonsky family whose old-fashioned wealthy lives seemed unshakeable at that time. Their grand houses in Moscow and Leningrad functioned effortlessly through the work done by a horde of invisible servants. This was how it had always been for the upper class in comfortably ossified Russia. But the coming war was about to overturn that.

After a few more pages of this engrossing story we were ready to walk again. We had chosen the next town, Fontevraud, as the place to stay overnight. There was no youth hostel but it was big enough for us to expect to find cheap rooms there. When we would get there we would have walked sixteen kilometres, and were proud when we worked that out

"There's a famous old Romanesque abbey there. I'm hoping we are going to have enough time to look around it today," John said.

We arrived at the outskirts in mid-afternoon, and as we walked down the main street running footsteps came up behind us.

"Excuse me. Can I help you?" A French teenager, breathless from hurrying, was calling to us [below, left]. We stopped and he caught up, a schoolboy of about sixteen, curly haired and open faced.

"You are pilgrims, aren't you? Are you looking for somewhere to eat? Do you need a place for to-night?" So many eager questions, quite unlike the way the French normally approached strangers.

"Yes, we are looking for a pension."

"I thought so. My brother and I wondered if you would stay with us. Our parents are away so we are on our own tonight. We would love you to join us." His words tumbled out eagerly as he pointed to a tall narrow old house across the main street.

By now his elder brother had caught up with us. Jean-Marie had just finished his second year at university [right on page 15]. Though he was more reserved he also eagerly joined his brother in urging us to stay with them that night. And so we gratefully accepted. As they introduced themselves they shook hands with each of us, including our children, in the traditional French style of that time.

They took us up the steep stairs into the house with talk flowing. "We have five elder sisters. They have all married and left home so there is plenty of spare room here," Jean-Marie told us.

Their father was the local hairdresser. "But we don't let him cut our hair," they stated firmly. Their bold long hair must surely challenge a barber in a quiet old-fashioned town. It was obvious the boys were bursting to move into a wider world and saw us as living out part of their dream.

"Tonight we are giving a dinner party to celebrate Jean-Marie's university results. He has done very well so we have invited two of our friends over. We were on our way to the horse butcher to buy steaks when we saw you."

"Uh!" said the girls in disgust. "We don't eat horse meat!"

Most Australians reacted to that thought although we had never tasted the meat. The boys were astonished.

"It's a luxury in France," they told us.

So John diplomatically said he would like the experience. We others asked for the thin French beef steaks we were familiar with.

While the boys went shopping we visited the famous Fontevraux Abbey at the end of the town. We were the only visitors, and were directed to the eastern chapel where we found a group of tombs of kings and queens. All of them had been rulers of England. Here were the tombs of King Henry II and two of his sons, King Richard I and King John. I wondered what were they doing here in France?

Beside them were Queen Blanche, the wife of King John, and his mother Queen Eleanor of Aquitaine.

I stopped and stared at the tomb of this woman lying quietly absorbed in a book. How composed she looked. Where did she fit among these bellicose men? What did I know about her?

Then it came back to me. She was lying close to her second husband, King Henry, and John and Richard were two of her sons. What else had I heard about her?

She had twice been queen, first of France and then of England, and in both a great administrator. These were two of her many

children and each in turn had reigned as a king of England, yet while in power they both deferred to her. She was a woman of great beauty and charisma and politically very powerful.

"These are English kings and queens. Why are they here in France?" Cassandra asked

"I'm not sure," John answered, "especially since Henry who was her second husband wanted nothing to do with Eleanor in his later life. She led their sons to war against him. He defeated them and imprisoned her for fifteen years. She was only released by Richard on Henry's death. So why were their bodies buried here? And another puzzle: Though these kings ruled England they were all actually born this side of the Channel."

Returning to the house we found the party ready to start. The other guests had arrived. They were close friends of the boys from school days. It was all a bit reserved at first, but our children soon thawed their formality.

The table was set with bottles of red wine and soft drinks for our children. The air was bright with celebration.

Talk quickly moved to politics.

"All of us are pacifists," Jean-Marie told us, challengingly. "You have seen our beautiful local forest. It's immense and enormously old. The army has got an idea that they can take it over for military manoeuvres!" He laughed angrily. The others grew equally intense.

"The whole town has tried to stop them," his friend cut in, "even the mayor and all the most conservative people. But they have had no effect. The army has gone ahead and cut down swathes of trees; and they keep doing it. No-one can stop them."

Our talk moved out wider till we were discussing the Vietnam war and the way colonial regimes had hung on to their colonies until they were finally challenged. It was lovely to find that young French people were passionately politically minded.

It was midnight before our talk ended and John and I climbed the rickety old staircase to bed.

3

CASSANDRA FINDS A DOLMEN

*When you plod, everything seems to take forever, and forever
is a lovely thing when you stop being scared of it. Strange how something that
takes a lot of time can give you a feeling
that there is a lot of time
and a lot of space and a good measure of ease.*
  Michael Leunig

Jean-Marie and Michel joined our walk next morning. They said
they would guide us out of town but I thought they also wanted a
taste of being pilgrims.

"Look out for the cave–houses up in the hills," Jean Marie told
us. "They are quite special. Our grandmother lived in one of them.
They are carved out of soft limestone, a type of sculpting."

John was very interested. "Yes I know about using limestone in
churches. It takes weeks and weeks for it to harden. And we came
across some cave houses in southern Italy."

Michel added, "They make really nice little houses. They always
keep the same temperature and they never leak."

This morning our path took us through a stretch of raw deforested land where the stumps still smelt of fresh resin. The boys pointed out the warning notices pinned up at regular intervals: "Attention! Do not step off the path. Regular military manoeuvres are carried out here." This was the army's presence.

Our friends turned home when we reached healthy forest again. "They'll attack this next," Jean-Marie said dejectedly.

Years later I met someone who said they knew Jean-Marie, an extraordinary coincidence. This person told me he had become a professor in a German university.

Recently I heard another story about French forests under threat: and how an Englishwoman working in Paris had not let dejection defeat her. One of the finest old forests in France was about to be destroyed; Permission had already been. It was not the army's doing this time, but for a Formula I car racing course.

Undeterred, she marched passionately past series of secretaries into the very office of the minister himself and, interrupting him, she pointed out that this destruction went against his own party's ideals. She was so certain in herself that she got him to reverse the decision. She saved her forest.

We had not walked much further when Cassandra spotted a little white cluster of caves up the hill in the distance.

"There they are," she said. "This was where their grandmother lived." They had told us no-one lived there any more, and these little homes were used for raising rabbits and ducks and storing garden tools. There was nothing more to see, and we passed on.

"Walking here is nothing like in Australia, is it?" Rebecca said. "At home the same scenery goes on for hours. Here it is different all the time."

I said, "I guess it would have been much the same in medieval times. But the roads would have been very different."

"And different again in the Roman times," John added. "Their roads were straight as an arrow so their troops could quickly move great distances. That was how they controlled their empire. After it collapsed no-one looked after the roads any more and they fell apart."

"The forests would have always been dense, with wolves and boars and bears living in them. Scary! Travellers must have been constantly on guard," I said.

"That's why pilgrims took staves. They also needed them against robbers and such people."

"But that would not have helped much against a ferocious wild animal, would it?" Emily warned.

Back then people's best protection was to travel in big groups. They would have been a mixture of merchants, clerics and masons as well as pilgrims. Some people's jobs took them far afield, even then.

When the Clunaic monasteries saw that lawless bands were attacking travellers on a big scale they began protecting them by building dormitories and hospices along the most popular routes. They also provided them with basic food and nursed the sick and buried those who died. One route was in the Pyrenees on the border between France and Spain, the monastery of Roncesvalle, now on the most popular camino route.

In medieval times the monks of Roncesvalle (as drawn on the left by Cassandra) would pray for the souls of pilgrims who died on the journey, from cold and hunger or being killed by wolves or thieves or by simply losing their way in the notorious mists of that remote mountain pass. Aware of such dangers the monks would regularly keep tolling a bell through the night.

The farmhouses we were passing south of Fontevraux were traditional homesteads with low stone out-buildings arranged around an open courtyard. We leaned on

the fence and admired the ducks and turkeys and hens as they freely wandered, digging insects out of rotting piles of manure and straw.

"Listen to that turkey," Emily said. "Gobble! Gobble! Gobble! Look at him strutting around displaying its feathers, going on just like a peacock."

"I like the ducks best," Becky said. "Look how their heads go down into the water."

"And the hens and chickens," said Cassandra. "Really I love them all. Listen to how they cluck and quack."

Because we were leading a homeless life, these long-established farms charmed us, and perhaps that was why we later in Australia put down our roots in a country spot.

Everyone passing wished us good day and were impressed by the children. "Little pilgrims," they said admiringly in recognition of what they saw.

Around this time Cassandra happily added another level to our pilgrimage. She had been interested in archaeological sites for a long while.

Cassandra: *I was fascinated by ancient dolmen and menhirs, and would search our maps for the symbols that marked their location. Whenever I could persuade everyone to walk the extra distance,*

we would detour and sit and explore their powerful and timeless stillness amidst the changing countryside around.

"There's a dolmen quite near us. Let's go and look at it, I so want to, and have never seen one."

Dolmen are ancient man-made structures of stone from pre-historic times. Little is known about them, even today. Years of study have only made it clear there was some deep ritualistic purpose behind the placing of the big flat stones. We don't know how they brought the stones great distances from far-off quarries, and set them upright to balance on top of each other.

The arrangements are thought to be connected with the phases of the moon and the sun, and even some stars.

Cassandra's excitement affected us all when we found the dolmen. It was one enormous slab as thick as Emily was tall, and balanced on top of three massive posts. All in unhewn granite. We clambered to the top of the pile and took photographs while she made sketches in her notebook. Dolmens were her own private road to explore; and years later she would study archaeology at university.

Our other social contacts during the day continued to be people working in the vineyards, groups of men and women filling baskets with grapes while their little children played in the grass. We waved and called out to each other as we passed.

Each time we moved onto a walking track or through sunny

open woods we took off our sandals to enjoy the sensuousness of bare feet on crisp crunchy leaves.

As we walked, I remembered being told that Napoleon had planted apple trees along highways to provide food for his troops. What extraordinary forethought. Were these some of them?

But in fact, it turned out they had a simpler origin. They had been planted by the villagers. Would they have minded us helping ourselves? After all, we only took a few.

While we were eating, the sky grew ominously dark.

"It's going to rain any minute," I said.

"It had better hold off till we get into town," John added.

It did, but we were weary when we got there, for we had walked twenty-two kilometres today. Our feet were very aware of it. They were sore and tired, as they would never be later. We had thought we were experienced walkers but this was pushing us way beyond what we were used to.

The town we had aimed for, Curcay-sur-Dive, turned out to be no more than a village, with no accommodation. So what were we going to do? Our plan of staying off main roads was going against us.

"We may have to do what we did when we were students hitching," John said, "and sleep on the school house veranda tonight. We did that often back then."

"But we don't have sleeping bags, and it's probably not OK to do this in France. People used to be easy-going about it in Australia, but that was in the nineteen forties. They might be unhappy about it here. And anyway we don't have any food."

We stood looking at the primary school and its lunch shed at the back and knew that was not our answer. But what else was there?

Just then a man appeared and in a voice of authority asked what we were doing here. We told him that we had walked all day and expected we would find accommodation in this village.

"You won't be able to stay here tonight," he said rather definitely as if he had been reading our minds. "You will have to go on to

Thouars. It's a big town. You will easily find somewhere there. And it's not far, only thirteen kilometres." Our spirits plummeted at these words. We couldn't walk that extra distance.

Then he added, "I am waiting for my wife to finish her work: she runs the primary school. I still have time to drive you there." Wondrous words, but we did manage to feel a little embarrassed.

As we squeezed into his car, bags and sticks and all, it was clear that he had no interest in our pilgrimage, so we talked of other matters. It seemed only a moment before he dropped us in a little square outside Saint-Laon in the old quarter of Thouars.

We felt this was the time and place to use Pére Robert's letter of introduction. The curé would direct us where to go.

The curé himself answered our knock and read our letter of introduction, while we waited silently.

His response was immediate and positive. "I can put you up here. Come in, come in," he said and took us into the rambling old manse. He searched out two of his fellow-priests and handed us over.

"I will see you tomorrow morning," he concluded.

At the top of a big staircase we were shown into two empty adjoining rooms. The two priests looking after us dragged in beds and hunted out blankets.

"We have our own sleeping sheets and towels," we told them.

We could see this was not the first time people had been dossed down here and we knew that pilgrims walking to Santiago had been put up by the Church for over a thousand years.

"There you are," said the older man comfortably. "And you can cook your dinner on the stove in our kitchen downstairs." We felt really enfolded.

The six priests who shared the building were looked after in their turn by a local woman who acted as their part-time housekeeper. She kept the house clean, shopped for them and once a week prepared basic dishes and left them in the refrigerator. They each ate separately and heated up the food when they chose. It was a casual way of life for hard–working priests, in contrast to the comfort and attractiveness we would later find in nunneries.

Our rooms were bare but the girls took happily to their one, quickly turning it into a playroom, while we went out to buy food. The thought of getting a glimpse of the old town while we shopped had re-energized us. This would be our play.

It was growing dark in the square, but the food shops were open. First we found a charcuterie, which is a world away from delicatessens at home. Its shop window was crowded with freshly home–made dishes temptingly arranged.

We hovered outside to examine them. "What about those little ham and onion pies? We could heat them in the oven. And some more cheese. What else do you think?"

At the greengrocer's we picked up fruit and potatoes. We wanted a solid meal. Meat was usually light on our menu at that time because of its cost, but vegetables made up for it. This parsimony led Emily later in the journey to defiantly announce to us all that she was a meatarian.

Back in the kitchen Brother Joseph was putting his meal together.

"I have to eat quickly," he said. "I have an appointment with two of my parishioners." He had a long program stretching into the evening.

"Each of us has our own group of village churches around Thouars to be in charge of," he explained.

We talked over the stove while we put our meals together. He was heating a packet soup and warming mashed potato from the refrigerator. He had ignored the sautéed kidneys and the carrots in white sauce. He finished his meal with milk pudding and slices of bread and jam; a limited meal for a busy man.

He was out of the door before we had finished cooking.

After our meal we shared another chapter of *War and Peace*.

4

THE RELUCTANT PILGRIM

Monks' feet clomping
Through the icy dark, drawing
Sweet water
  Basho

Next morning the curé showed us through his church. We were charmed by its Romanesque western doorway and by the exterior, but found the interior a shock of disappointment. For at some later date a heavy hand had restored it in such a way as to rob it of its original simplicity.

Another visitor had been here some eight hundred years before: the formidable Abbot Bernard of Clairvaux, a man few could oppose.

He had been disappointed too, but for a different reason. The original west front of the church that we were admiring had soured him. He was highly critical of the ornamentation around the portals.

"What profit is there in these ridiculous monsters, to what purpose are those unclean apes, those fierce lions, those monstrous centaurs?" he demanded. Despite his protests, the spectacular ornamentation has remained intact to this day.

When we were leaving we expected to pay the curé for our stay but he would not hear of it. "Then let us give a donation for the church?"

"No, no. You are pilgrims; that is enough."

In fact he had been thinking of how to help us further, for he told us he had rung the nuns at Airvault on our behalf.

"Saint Agnes is our local girls' boarding school. It is in the next town and on your way. I thought they would be interested to hear what you are doing so I rang them and they have asked you to stay to-night."

We were delighted. To be in a Catholic girls' boarding school would be a special experience. We did not think of enquiring how far it was, but later discovered it was twenty-four kilometres. We had not thought of walking so far in a day, though later we would travel much longer distances with pleasure.

But there was no accommodation closer. We were on the back roads. Reflecting on yesterday's near-disaster, I wonder that John and I did not immediately decide we should move onto busier roads. If we had been quicker learners we would have missed our most precious experiences.

Nevertheless, as we set out today our feet protested. Long regular days of walking were more than they were used to.

At the start of the pilgrimage we had been most conscious of our packs for they were old-style simple ones, the kind that had no supportive metal frames resting on the hips. But we were now at home with them. It was our feet that were holding our attention.

One of the girls said in a disgruntled tone, "People talk about putting your best foot forward. What do they mean? Both mine hurt equally!"

But we never developed blisters, though today's pilgrims complain a lot about them. I think that may have been because we had often gone barefoot, or because our soft shoes melded into the irregularities of the path. Many people find the first days of

a pilgrimage testing because the endless walking challenges the pattern of most normal lives.

   We were at the point where we were getting tired. This pilgrimage was asking much of us, and Emily's spirits began to sag. She was facing the real nature of a pilgrimage. It was turning into an unremitting walk. There was not going to be enough time for play.

Emily was still a long way from being a teen-ager. She had not yet picked up that extra level of resilience the others had come to. So when she got into a hard situation she drew on her obstinacy; but today the stubborn streak that had often been a support turned against her. To make sure we were aware of her painful feet and her even more painful feelings she now took on a resentful shuffle.

The girls could not but notice and, fortunately for us, Cassandra provided a distraction.

"Look at that tree," she said, "Someone's painted stripes on it." Two neat red lines with an arrow below them were painted at eye height on the trunk.

"That is a *sentier* mark," I exclaimed, "how exciting! They are painted by a club of walkers to lead you through the most beautiful regions of France. You won't always find them because some farmers don't like people going through their properties so they deliberately wipe them off."

Cassandra couldn't wait. "Come on Em, let's look for the next one." When Emily found the next sign, now happy and eager, she exclaimed, "It's like a peanut hunt." She was happy again, that restored all of us.

The path was taking us through lovely countryside where grand old houses in generous grounds stood well back from the road. Their shutters were blindly closed. Perhaps families only came there for holidays, for they carried a quality of eternally waiting to be visited.

At the end of the afternoon we came back onto the main road. We were all tired by now. Although John was carrying Emily's pack, she hardly had enough spirit for the last few kilometres. We had all grown quiet.

We had stopped for another rest when we saw a car approaching.

"Let's hitch-hike!" one of us said, and waved. Hitchhiking was still a new experience for the girls: they really liked the idea. To our joy and amazement the car pulled up smartly and a door was thrown open.

"Saint Agnes?" the man said. "I am going there now. I am their doctor. Hop in." How fortuitous! Our relief was so great we bounded into his car, squashed and happy.

Perhaps it seems surprising that local people were so ready to go out of their way to help us, but hitch-hiking was accepted at that time – and having children helped.

Saint Agnes was a big solid dark brick building with ample space for its four hundred boarders and staff. As the doctor went about his own business, we rang the front bell.

A nun opened the door. "Come in," she said, smiling, "Mother Superior is expecting you," and led us to her tiny office. We were quite a crowd in there.

Mother Superior spoke warmly, "We have been looking out for you," she said. She was an attractive young woman in her thirties and clearly in command.

"It is fortunate you have arrived at the end of the week," she said, "or we could not have fitted you in. This afternoon our weekly boarders went home for the weekend, so their beds are empty."

After more talk she said, "Sister Madeleine will show you to your rooms. Would you like to have a bath before dinner?"

"Yes," we all said together, and with feeling.

Sister Madeleine led us down a hall to an empty dormitory where our beds had been prepared. On the way we had occasional glimpses of pupils. They were obviously as interested in us as our

children were to see them. It was a pity there was no thought of
giving them a chance to meet.

We did not have to take turns for a bath, as there were enough
for us all. The gift was very special at this stage in our walk. We
lazed in the hot water, and soaked away layers of tiredness.

A traditional French dinner was royally served to us in the staff
dining room, one small course after another brought by two of the
nuns. A tureen of clear vegetable soup was followed by an entrée
of cold meats. After a delicious macaroni and fish dish came the
traditional cheese board and lastly a big bowl of fruit. There was red
wine for John and me and fizzy drink for the girls, and of course the
crisp freshly baked loaves that are always part of any French meal.

We relished it all and were more than replete when we went to
bed. There was no thought of reading Tolstoy tonight.

But John and I did find a moment for a private word with the
nuns who had served us. Like us they were concerned with Emily's
weariness. She was still on the verge of tears, shadow-eyed and
limping after the long walk today. Not many children of her age
could have done it. But unlike the nuns, we were also aware that
her obstinacy was still inducing her to occasionally make her point
by walking in a way that was making it much worse. We wanted to
help her drop it.

The nuns came up with a good suggestion.

"Tomorrow is Saturday. A train stops at our station to take the
local people to a market town further down the line. If you took
it you would move on restfully. You will also avoid the rain we
are expecting!" A great idea! We had not had rain up to now, but
the rain was to start next day and would cloud our journey for the
following week.

"Then we will call you for an early breakfast," they said.

5

WHERE CAN YOU GO ON A SATURDAY NIGHT?

I felt I was sharing in the medieval life as the rhythm of the day
was set by our own footsteps, slow and steady
   Rebecca

It was still dark when the early-morning knock came on our door.

"Up quickly! We are taking a train!"

We could hear rain falling. This was what we half- expected, but still it was depressing.

The nun who served our breakfast had a more positive attitude to the day, but she was not thinking of the rain when she said, "It is fortunate you are leaving to-day. A strike begins tomorrow and we have no idea how long it will last."

So we would have to deal with the strike, on top of the continual rain and Emily's tiredness. What would be next? Yet we weren't really surprised at this news. At that time strikes had become part of daily life in France.

Still, we had a train today. That was what mattered. And in spite of its strikes, we liked the French railway system. It was much cheaper than British Rail since the government was not making a profit from it. It was also wonderfully flexible and imaginative, shaping itself around local needs like this. Today it was providing a small two-car train to take people to the nearby Saturday market. Not many people in France could afford cars at that time.

When we arrived at the market town it was still raining. So we boldly transferred to another little train to attempt to get beyond the rain, going a hundred kilometres further south.

Today the orthodox approach is to walk all the way to Santiago, or to ride if you are going on horseback or by bicycle. It did not occur to us that we should all be suffering more than we were. After all, this was forty years ago when so few were on the camino, and there were no rules or expectations that we knew of.

We had come to feel comfortable with mainly walking, while including short hitch-hikes and a few train rides wherever they helped us out of difficulties. This was not a competitive trip, just a rich experience for ourselves. Our family's needs came first.

After a restful morning on the train, we were all singing when we walked down the road. Then Cassandra pulled up. She had just seen a bird on the ground. It was crouching, frightened, and when she came up to it, was so submissive it actually allowed her to pick it up.

She gently examined it all over.

"It doesn't seem to be hurt at all. Maybe it was tired and having a rest when a car passed over it and gave it a shock?"

"It might have been part of a big flock but dropped out when it was tired; or perhaps it's just a tired old bird."

We could only guess at its story.

There was some milk left from lunch, so Cassandra made bread and milk to feed it. When we moved on, she carried it on one hand as she walked, talking to it softly. In a short time it revived so well that it was able to flex its wings; and a moment later it took off.

"I wonder where it's going?" Rebecca said. "It seems to know its way. Will it catch up with the others?"

"Remember the bird I bought for you in Bali, Cass?" Emily said. "It got well again quickly too."

"Yes it did, even though the boys wouldn't have treated it well."

At the time, Emily had been walking through our village looking for a birthday present for Cassandra when she came across two Balinese boys carrying a bird. Seeing her interest, they quickly offered to sell it to her. She managed to trade it for two of the local plastic bangles she was wearing and came home triumphant.

But that bird didn't stay long either. As soon as it recovered, it too flew away.

A burst of pursuing rain cut short these memories and we sheltered under a large tree. When we moved on, the sky was still doubtfully grey. "This may keep on happening," John said. "After all, it is autumn." He had hardly said this when a heavier downpour chased us into a barn.

We were not sure if the owners would like us being there, for the French have a strong sense of privacy. Fortunately no one came by.

As we settled on hay bales we found our book and read some more from *War and Peace*; and I relaxed, glad we no longer had a stressed bird travelling with us. Our lives were full enough without it.

Although the rain cleared quickly again, we decided to speed up our travel to the next town with further hitchhiking.

We were quickly rewarded. A local man took us the last eight kilometres into Aulnay.

John had said trustingly, "The handbook says this hostel is open all year."

We had no trouble finding it. But a notice was pinned on the door, announcing plainly, in English, French and German, that the hostel had closed down, permanently. Such a letdown!

A passer-by, seeing us clustered despondently, gave us new heart. He told us of a modest guesthouse nearby

"But it is the only one," he added. We were not as confident this time as we hunted for it; and rightly as it turned out.

For when we got there it had its own notice pinned up, this time with just one word: "Complet". Once there would have been spaces but we had come too late. It was Saturday night and everyone had come into town. To make the situation worse, the rain had returned. So much for our long train trip to avoid it!

We saw no answer but to turn to the church again.

I knocked on the door of the manse. No answer. I knocked again, this time longer, though less confidently.

A neighbour looked over the fence. "The curé is not at home. He is holding a wedding on the other side of town."

"Can you help us? We are looking for a cheap place for the night? The guest house is full."

"No. There is nowhere else in Aulnay, except the big hotel." So we had come to the end of the road. Even a big town had nothing to offer us. It was no better than little Curcay-sur-Dive. Except perhaps in one possibility, the local priest.

So we sat down to wait for the curé to return. Fortunately the rain had again been brief.

While the rest of us sprawled wearily on the stones at the west door of the church, John, still vigorous, wandered off.

He came back a moment later, elated. "This is a wonderful old church from the first half of the twelfth century. I have worked out it was built very quickly, and then left virtually untouched for the

next eight hundred years. It's a perfectly preserved example of a small parish church of that period. I'm going to take some photos."

"By the way," he added, "It was built in Eleanor of Aquitaine's time. We are in her duchy, where she lived as a child." John was enjoying himself.

It was a long time before the curé arrived. When he did, I saw a tired man approaching and wondered how he would feel to find five strangers wearily settled outside his door. I wished we didn't have to bother him.

"Normally it would be no problem putting you up," he said when we explained our predicament, "but I have just lent a dozen spare mattresses for a wedding party."

He stood thinking. He was not going to turn us away easily, it was not in his nature or training. Instead he brought us inside, out of the next drizzle, which had become a hovering companion always just around us this day.

We stood awkwardly at attention while he began hunting through his spare room.

"Ah!" he exclaimed triumphantly. In a far corner he had come across two big mattresses and some thick eiderdowns.

"How fortunate! I did not know these were here." We all relaxed and introduced ourselves. Up to this point we had been no more than an awkward problem. Now we could meet on another footing. We discovered that his name was Father Pierre.

"Australians!" he said of us with new interest. A friendship was about to start.

Between us we carried the bedding into a pleasant empty room, gave it a shake and spread it under the windows.

"You will be comfortable here," he said, satisfied. "The bathroom is just down the hall, and you are welcome to use my kitchen."

And so we gratefully started settling in. Time to make up another temporary home. The food we had bought earlier turned into an ample meal to share with our host.

Over dinner he questioned us keenly about life in Australia and we found that he, like so many others in France at that time, knew little about our country. We also talked about our experiences so far on the camino.

After the meal he turned on the television to listen to the world news and we were startled to learn that a war had broken out in the Middle East. Over these last days when we had been absorbed in our personal lives, in the bigger world Egypt and Syria had made a surprise attack on Israel.

It happened on Yom Kippur Day, the holiest day of the Jewish year, so it caught Israel off–guard. For most the army was off–duty, praying at home or in the synagogues. To add to the surprise of the situation, Yom Kippur Day this year occurred during the Moslems' holy month of Ramadan. The Arabs too would have been expected to have been equally absorbed in their religious duties.

In those days we automatically considered that Israel would have been the victim in any situation with their Arab neighbours, as did Father Pierre. Today the relationship between Israel and the Arab countries is very different; there is more aggression on the Jewish side than the Arab's.

After the curé turned off the television set, we were talking about the war when a motorbike roared up to the door. A tall robust young

man flung himself into the room, his loud cheerful voice entering ahead of him. Energetically he filled the room.

Casually cutting across our talk, he spoke directly to the curé, shouting as if across a valley. We could not understand his accent but noticed that Father Pierre answered him briefly and very quietly. The young man nodded then took himself off to another part of the house. He did not glance at us.

The girls and I went to bed while John stayed on, talking. Later John told me that Father Pierre had talked at length about his work, saying "There are not enough priests in France today, so we are all overworked. I have twelve churches under my care. How can I tend to my parishioners properly? Yet I am expected to."

We had heard this story before. On one occasion we had met a priest of eighty who was still responsible for all his parishes, and there were over a dozen. He could not retire because there was no one to replace him.

Father Pierre also explained how the young man came to be living in his house. The man was so mentally unbalanced he was not capable of living on his own. When he was a baby his mother had put him into foster care soon after birth and then he had been constantly moved from one foster mother to another. This threw off the balance of his mind.

There was nowhere else in the parish to send him, so Father Pierre and another priest shared the responsibility. He lived in turn between their houses. That way each of them had some respite from his shouting company. This was a not uncommon story of a priest being expected to do what we would expect a government department would do today.

"So who supports the priests?" I wondered.

John did not come to bed till very late that night.

6

THE SUNDAY HUNTERS

No hat and cold
Rain falling –
Well!
  Basho

Father Pierre had a surprise for us this morning.

"You have been invited to stay with a friend of mine tonight," he said. "Christian is a Lutheran pastor in Saint Jean-d'Angely, the next town you will come to."

We were having a relaxed breakfast, enjoying Father Pierre's company. The loud young man had not reappeared.

We would be walking nineteen kilometres today; by now we knew we could manage that, even though it was squalling, quite heavily. This regular rain was becoming too much of a pattern for our liking. Were we the West Wind in the *Hitchhiker's Guide to the Galaxy*, bringing rain with us wherever we went?

Not a comfortable thought, as our wind-jackets were not ging to be sturdy enough to keep this drenching rain out.

Father Pierre was a capable man and sought to support us. He hunted once more through his useful spare room and dug out four plastic sheets. These passed onto us.

We waited for a gap between two showers to leave, then waved goodbye to our new friend. By now John had permanently put most of the contents of Emily's pack into his. Freed of extra weight she was dancing along, as carefree as a bird.

Frequently walking through bursts of rain during the day did not prove easy. Rebecca wrote about it in her next letter.

It was really windy and the wind kept trying to tug our plastics away. Mum and Emily were sharing a plastic. Emily pulled it so her knapsack was utterly uncovered. When we covered it, the wind caught it and blew it off again.

We had not gone more than three or four kilometres when the rain returned in a downpour. We sheltered under a big protective tree, covering four of the knapsacks with the largest plastic then using the other three to shelter us, by squashing as close together as we could. We weren't shivering because the rain did not chill us.

In fact we all felt hearty today. Rebecca wrote,

It was great fun walking along with the rain going pitter-patter on our plastics, trying to keep as much of our jeans and knapsacks dry as possible. Whenever it began to rain heavily we would shelter in barns or under trees. And then the sun would come out again.

What is it that can shift a problem into being a challenge, and a challenge into being an adventure? We came to a hamlet with a tiny church, open and empty, so we hurried inside. "This is the perfect place to have lunch," I said, "as long as we do it neatly," But before we had had a chance to settle down on the pews and pull out packages, a middle-aged woman suspiciously followed us in and indignantly drove us out. We might well have been her hens the way she spoke to us. Oh well!

Around another bend and still in the hamlet, a small bar materialized. What a rare and happy find! There was smoke coming

out of the chimney.Inside was a thickly masculine world, a small dark room crowded with men absorbed in a noisy game of cards. Around the roaring log fire they had draped their parkas to dry. They were local farm hands who had started the day with dogs and guns as Sunday hunters. Then they too had been held back by the rain.

They were of all ages and had glasses of wine beside them and their big damp hunting dogs pressing close. Emily was delighted at this and in a minute was down amongst them. As she stroked them, their long tails beat responsively on the floor.

The men looked up from their cards, greeting us in the traditional manner. "Bonjour Monsieur, Madame, Demoiselles."

Not an automatic greeting, but with warmth for fellow travellers in the rain. Everyone was especially sympathetic when they saw how drenched we were. We laughed together over it. The bar tender helped us stow our packs and staves out of the way, then put our wind jackets to dry; and everyone moved over a little to share the space by the fire. It was so cheering.

In bars at that time it was acceptable to unpack your own bits of food and eat, as long as you ordered a drink. So we ordered hot drinks for us all and then unpacked our bits.

Looking at the guns, I remembered an earlier experience I had had of Sunday hunting.

I had been reading peacefully in our cottage in Chartres when a bullet came through the open window. It came in from the woods and lodged into the wall behind me. And if it had hit me no-one would have been the wiser. Another bird down!

In France each Sunday in autumn the countryside was filled with the ring of guns. In the markets we saw their trophies, the naked bodies of little birds on the stalls and we had grieved for them. Each bird was no more than a morsel. Too little to be sacrificed like that. As I looked over at the guns and I could not help feeling glad their purpose had been halted for now.

Eventually the rain eased and the hunters and their dogs

disappeared. We had an easy last stretch into Saint Jean-d'Angelay.

Even John did not know that this town had a rich pilgrimage history. We only discovered years later the importance of the Royal Abbey that had been built in the ninth century to hold the precious relic, the head of Saint John the Baptist.

In the Middle Ages pilgrims had a deep mystical belief in relics. They became the greatest draw-card any church could collect. It was of no concern to believers that the same relic often was held in several places. Crowds of pilgrims flocked to the Royal Abbey and gave generously to get protection from Saint John himself.

In time the abbey fell into ruins and in 1973 had still not been restored; though it has since then.

Christian lived in a small modern apartment opening onto an outside staircase. Because the Lutherans of France were modestly endowed, they possessed no grand church or manse.

We knocked and a tall blonde young man promptly opened the door. "Come in, come in," he called hospitably. "You must be the Australian family." He looked undeterred by five wet visitors crowding through his doorway.

In the living room racks of wet washing were steaming round the heater and the air was loud with the fretful crying of small children. In spite of his positive voice it seemed we had come at a bad moment. Not even our arrival had deterred the solid determined voice of his two-year-old daughter, though his four-year-old son stopped midway and looked at us with interest. Christian seemed young to be the father of these children and a pastor.

He hospitably urged us to add our wet garments to his rack.

"My wife is not at home this evening," he said apologetically. "She is a nurse and is on night shift now, and I am looking after the family. Anne-Marie is very fretful as she is teething."

Rebecca loves little children. As she went over and started talking to Ann-Marie the crying stopped. The other girls joined them.

We were glad to have brought a supply of food to contribute, as this was Sunday afternoon when all the shops of France are closed.

The eight of us were eating the rice dish we had jointly created round the dining-room table when I asked Christian if he had always lived in this town. "No! I moved here because of its Lutheran congregation."

He told us Saint Jean–d'Angely had a long Protestant history, going back before the religious civil war when the Huguenots were defeated by the Catholics. That was when the abbey and its church were burned down. I told him that my mother's ancestors, the Le Souef family, had been French Huguenots. They had left Normandy and fled to England and later emigrated to Australia.

An evening full of talk, but the present war in the Middle East did not come into our conversation.

As we were going to bed, Christian told us we would have to leave very early because Saintes was a long way off and there would be nowhere for us to stay before then. "I am sad we won't meet your wife. But do thank her too," I said as we parted.

7

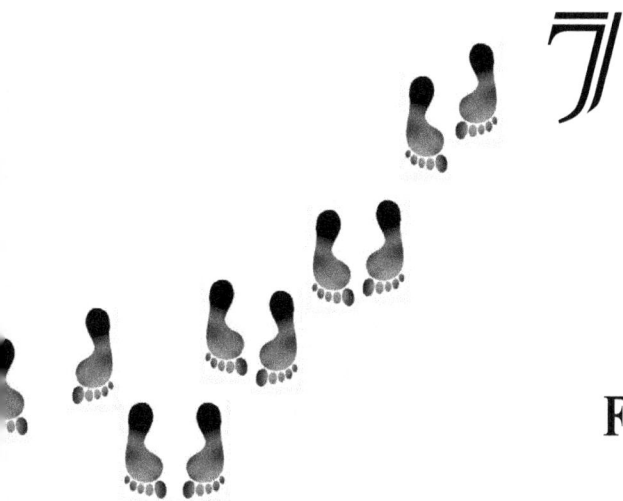

FURTHER SOUTH

Go to the end of the path until you get to the gate
Go to the gate and head straight out towards the horizon.
Keep going towards the horizon.
Sit down and have a rest now and again,
But keep on going, just keep on with it.
Keep on going as far as you can.
That's how you get there.
  Michael Leunig

We crept out early next morning with a long way to go, knowing that Christian's wife had come home late in the night and the family was still asleep.

The city of Saintes was tonight's destination. We would be moving away from the simple back-roads into sophisticated suburbia. Our guidebook told us confidently that its youth hostel stayed open all year, but we had read those words before! Yet if we were turned way again, we knew we would have some choice in a big town.

In spite of yesterday's rain, the grass was dry when we stopped for breakfast. So afterwards we optimistically packed away our plastic sheets, along with our mugs and plates.

A lot of things looked different this morning. Whitewashed stone cottages had grape-vines clambering over them; and the local people spoke with an interesting pronounced accent that we found hard to understand. We had moved into the Languedoc in southern France, where the climate was different and so were the culture and the spirit of the people.

It was at this point that we met another pilgrim. Cassandra is the only one who remembers this brief meeting. The rest of us doubted her memory until I came across a record in two photographs. They were of a young man, be-spectacled and with a very small beard and a bulky pack on his back. He was walking companionably beside our children. How could the rest of us have forgotten him? I can only think that our time together had been brief and uneventful.

Nowadays it is a different experience for pilgrims. They join the camino at any point they choose and are immediately part of a pilgrim community. There will always be some ahead of them and others coming behind. All are heading for the same inner goal, Santiago de Compostela. All are moving in that direction. They even have to vie for available beds at night. But though they are having much the same outer experiences, they absorb them differently.

It is the inner journey that matters for each of them, and this is never the same. The only thing everyone has in common is that none of them will view their lives quite the same after they have been through the experience.

Though our children were young enough to be taking our travels lightly, they too have been stamped by the experience. They have gladly held onto the memories of this experience even though we were not closely joined to any common pilgrim path.

This, our only fellow-pilgrim on this whole long journey, was not part of our walk for long. We must have parted from him before we thought it was time for lunch.

As we came upon a farm on the outskirts of a village I suggested, "Let's buy some milk." We had done this frequently in the past. It had never been an issue with farmers, so we unpacked our billycan confidently and unlatched the garden gate.

A crowded group was eating their midday meal under a huge oak tree. They were gathered round a long table outside the farmhouse, the farmer and his family, and a dozen or more of their workers.

We warmed to the sight of that table stocked with wine glasses and bottles of dark red gleaming wine, and platters piled with good food, a cheery country scene that could have come out of an Impressionist painting. The French have always known how to have good meals. They appreciate quality in food and especially relish savouring a meal together.

But this time it turned out we were intruding. We were breaking up an idyll. When we produced our billycan and asked to buy milk, the farmer's wife, a well built woman in her forties, stood up in her large apron and told us firmly. "No. Certainly not! We are having dinner."

In France no one, absolutely no one, is allowed to interrupt a midday dinner. Since those days we have made this blunder on a couple of unfortunate occasions. Each time the reaction to us has been strong and angry. It is definitely not done!

We looked around the table. All the others were looking at us, silently, unsmiling. She spoke for them all, and closed her words with a firm "Bonjour" that sent us apologetically on our way, feeling the sudden loneliness that comes from an unexpected rejection.

We were glad to find a village further on. Here we were able to fill our billycan with fresh water from an ancient well in the town square. Only after we had slowly pushed the stiff resistant old pump handle did the water start to gush out. It was refreshingly cold.

We settled by he pump under an apple tree, and savoured its perfectly ripe fruit with our meal. As we munched we watched a different traditional scene being played out in front of us.

A group of men were playing boule on a neatly laid out court.

Often we had watched this game but these players were particularly skilful. They were slow and concentrated, and most elegant in their movements. With an under-arm toss they guided their ball as close to the pic as possible.

Emily and Becky were full of talk, and absorbed in the game, but Cassandra only wanted to rest. She was the one who was tired and dejected today. We did not stay long, as we were mindful of the distance still ahead.

It was growing dark and the rain had come back when we finally got to Saintes. So much for packing away the plastics! As we hurriedly pulled them out, Rebecca said, "We will have to get an extra one to-morrow. We each need our own." She was right.

The hostel turned out to be on the far side of the city. We felt wet and soggy from the rain, light as it was, and opulently waved down a taxi!

It was a relief to see the hostel's blazing lights and the warden sitting at his desk ready to book us in. After a mixed day, everything was now in our favour, for there were plenty of empty beds.

"How many nights are you staying?" the warden asked. Hearing the rain outside, one of us said, "What if we make it three nights?" "Yes, definitely," everyone agreed. "And we can make it more if we have to."

"Good idea," the warden said. "This weather is only going to get worse. It is not just a local storm. On the news they said it has spread over the whole of southern Europe."

If we were in the hands of the gods, they were now on our side. We had found a snug haven at the perfect time and could stay here as long as we chose.

OUT OF THE RAIN

Winter downpour
Even the monkey
Needs a raincoat
　Basho

No need to get up early today. We had nothing to do and nowhere to go; a delicious feeling. We didn't care if it rained all day.

When we finally met downstairs, I was glad to find seven or eight young men and women were already having breakfast in the spacious old kitchen.

The girls were totally impressed by a young American, who called himself Chuck, sitting in a corner strumming on a guitar.

Rebecca: *He plays his guitar awfully well. He has been learning it for five years and says he hated it for the first two because it was so hard to learn. Cassy thinks this is a bit dampening since she's planning to learn.*

John and I had to go into the rain to pick up milk and croissants and a crunchy baguette for breakfast. We found we weren't the only dripping reluctant shoppers. None of us intended staying out a moment longer than we had to. How long would this rain go on for?

Looking for an answer to that question, we bought a French newspaper. Back in the kitchen everyone wanted to share its news. Once we had made bowls of milk coffee and hot chocolate, we read the weather news aloud, helped when we got stuck by our French fellow-hostellers. We found the warden had not been exaggerating. There was wild weather all through Europe and no suggestion of when it would ease. In fact it was far worse in other areas than here. There were floods in Nice while on the north coast of Spain several people in a fishing village had been drowned.

We were all very grateful that this hostel was open.

For the rest of the day we stayed snug in the living room, writing letters home.

Emily: *We are staying in a youth hostel to wait till the rain stops and to rest our weary feet. The first few days our feet hurt really madly. One night we stayed at a nunnery and when I got up after dinner I just about fell on my face my feet ached so.*

Rebecca: *It's gorgeous walking, and we have found things like wild figs, apples and walnuts, and birds stunned by cars. At the moment it is pouring with rain and as we have only plastics to protect our packs with, we have stopped at a youth hostel until it lets up. This morning the water was six inches deep in the street outside.*

Next morning we pulled ourselves away from this comfort to go to the post office. The children came too as we were all eager to get some mail.

"Any letters for the James family?" we asked at the post restante desk. The man shuffled through the J's then handed one over. It was for the girls, a letter from John's father, Jimmy as we called him.

"No more," I said hopefully? He shook his head. But we had one, and Jimmy's letters were precious. His fine Italic hand made them a joy to look at. Being an artist, he always added quirksical pictures to amuse the girls. We grouped round to hear it read aloud.

Dear Cassy, Becky and Em

I do feel I should write you each a letter in return for your last letters, which I do love getting, but I am a little bit pushed for time, so you will all have to do with just this one. Well! What times you do have! I imagine you "suffering" a good deal on your walking tour. Thus:

RAIN

MORE RAIN

MOUNTAINS, WITH MORE RAIN

FOREST, WITH MORE RAIN

MEALS, WITH RAIN

MORE MEALS, WITH MORE RAIN

DUCKS – QUITE HAPPY & WE KNOW WHY.

I do hope I'm wrong!
Well, maybe I am, & you are exhausted from getting too hot walking in the SUN!

And happily finishing with
Love from Jimmy
And from everybody here in Positano,
Back in the hostel the heavy weather had brought all the inmates
together. Most were young adults, and all were hitchhikers.

We laughed and talked, played cards and sang with the guitar.
The girls quickly made friends, loving hanging out with a crowd.
John and I needed this social change too. On top of that, we had
no plans to make and no uncertainties to solve. It was such a treat.

When Emily saw a young German called Klaus get out a chess
set she offered to play with him. He was surprised and, quietly,
quite impressed.

He set out the pieces and they sat opposite each other. A few
moves later I heard him, saying, quite shocked, "You can't do that."

"Why not?" Emily was blithe. She had picked up a few moves.
That was enough for her. From then on she was ready to be creative
and wildly free-flowing. Their chess game was short.

When a few of us were cooking in the hostel kitchen we
discovered that none of the others had heard about the pilgrim route
to Santiago. So we started sharing our experiences. Each of us was
eager to fill in any gaps the others left.

As we spoke of its ancient tradition, we were not aware that
Saintes too was full of its history. Only recently I read about it.

At the end of the eleventh century the monks rebuilt an enormous
abbey, Saint Eutrope, naming it after an early bishop. They also
built a priory, to care for the streams of pilgrims passing through.

The basilica had long been a ruin by the 1970's. But the crypt
where the relic of Saint Eutrope remained, still attracting pilgrims
and their gifts. Since then the church has been restored.

We did not go seeking history in that rain. But we did stumble on
a little local history which Cassandra wrote about:

*Yesterday as we struggled down the road to the post office to
send off our letters we were nearly drowned by the deluging rain.*

But it still felt a satisfying adventure. This is a lovely town, with its canals and museums. It is full of Roman and Medieval remains.

Mum and Dad and I have just come back from looking at an exhibition of peasant costumes and head-dresses and old furniture in a Folk Museum. It was great! We were led over the museum by a tiny old woman who showed us little bone flasks and some objects carved by sailors at sea.

Rebecca and Emily preferred to stay back in the hostel, playing cards with two young women they had made friends with, hopefully agreeing on the rules.

That evening Jean-Francois made crepes for us all. He had been rummaging through the communal cupboard of spare food supplies when he came across a packet of flour. He already had some eggs and I added another.

We gathered round. "I've got a lemon," Amanda said. "We could put lemon and sugar on them; and there's jam in the cupboard too."

That turned into a joyous time. We laughed as we tossed the crepes into the air, even when they came down in a folded mess.

John asked if any of them had heard that war had just broken out in the Middle East. No one had, nor were they interested. It seemed far away and detached from their happy lives.

So we passed the time until on the third day the rain grew intermittent and on the fourth morning we woke to a cloudless sky.

"It's time to go," was everyone's opinion.

(9)

SNIFFING COGNAC

Our walk was one of those pivotal destiny points in my life that changed me totally, so I was never to be the same again. It was a walk of pure magic, whatever the weather, an amazing journey. We set out with few things and lots of trust, and we were lucky that John and Hilary approached life in the same light-hearted way.

Cassandra

Everyone was leaving the hostel, but no one was going in our direction. "Goodbye, goodbye," we called.

Travellers have to expect short relationships with companions as we link up, enjoying whatever is in the here and now.

Now that the sun was shining we wanted to be quickly off into the countryside, and in our urgency we did not remember to hunt out another sheet of plastic to add to our raincoats. We did not consider walking out of town: it was too large, with industries on the outskirts, so we hunted out the railway station and caught another one-carriage train to Cognac. That twenty-minute train trip would save us a day of walking through flat uninteresting green fields squelchy with rain. We were constantly ensuring that our walks kept the children's interest, so that the experience would continue to be a rich one.

The other hostellers had suggested we call on one of the Cognac factories and have a tour of inspection as they had done. We were so glad they suggested this, as we would never have thought of it. It turned out there were four or five factories to choose from, and when we walked into the first we came across we were warmly welcomed and handed over to a guide who gave us a fascinating morning.

Our guide told us that French vineyards were originally created by the Romans in the third century. Distilled wines were not invented until the seventeenth century, he said, because delicate wines did not travel well over rough seas. I did not learn how they managed to overcome this problem at a later time since ships were still struggling over rough seas.

In 1907 the French government defined the area in which cognac could be grown and in 1939 they tightened it further, saying that cognac could only be grown in a specific geographical area which they judged by its soil. Today all the stages of growing cognac are carefully regulated to protect the industry.

Making cognac is a very slow process. All the casks come from one local oak forest, chosen for the high qualities of its timber. Its oaks thrive on its earth and the local water.

After the trees have been felled, they are left to season for seven years. Only then are they ready to be coopered into casks. It is the tannin that comes off cognac that gives it its distinctive taste.

The factories have to take great precautions against fire because the air inside the warehouses is heavy with perfume from the cognac's casks, making them very flammable. It smelt delicious to us but we could imagine it would be a heady place to be working in.

Their most precious and costly cognac goes directly into bottles, beautifully labelled and protectively packed.

In the tourist office on our way out, we nearly had a catastrophe.

Rebecca casually leaned her staff against the wall and then forgot it. We had gone some way down the road before she missed it.

"My stick!" she exclaimed.

The girls' staves were a close part of all our lives and we reacted immediately. As we swung around in consternation, we saw a woman from the tourist office hurrying towards us, the stick in her hand. Rebecca ran to meet her.

This never happened again.

The town of Cognac lies on the banks of the clear sparkling River Charente. We had come into a very smart region of France. We walked all afternoon past elegant well-tended properties with groves of pines and oaks. Here we found another dolmen, the finest one we had seen yet.

Our plan for that night was to stay in Jarnac but it was too small to put us up; but it did have a church and a helpful priest who knew exactly where to take us. He drove us seven kilometres down the road to the grand old Abbey of Bassac which he told us has

sheltered pilgrims through the Middle Ages.

This was a grand solid old building, parts of it dating back to the twelfth century. It delighted and amazed us,

The abbot himself came to the door when we knocked. He was a rugged burly man around fifty, with the practical manner of someone who was regularly involved in the world.

He read Father Robert's letter attentively.

"You are an architect. How fortunate you have come here. Come in, come in."

He led us down the passage saying, "We have been restoring this fine old place over the last twelve years. The whole place was allowed to run down for a very long time. After you have settled down I would like to show you what we have been doing."

Before he passed us over to one of his monks, he could not resist showing us the recently restored chapel we were passing. Several lovely modern stained glass windows had joined the old ones.

We dropped our bags in our bare and unadorned rooms, and were taken to dinner.

The dining-room was still in the original refectory. They needed all that space for the crowd of people already sitting on long trestle tables. There were monks, and also men from the building teams permanently at work on the abbey. The many grape-pickers were only here for seasonal work and looked tired after their long day in the boiling sun.

The abbot placed us beside him so we could continue our

conversation whilst we ate our meal. John talked of Chartres and how he thought the builders used to work, with master masons who could read latin and write, who were experts in the practical geometry used to create the templates that guided all the workemen on the building site.

After dinner, everyone helped clear up. The abbot washed up for our table while we helped two monks dry and put away.

They were very interested to meet Australians and were, like the others we had met, full of questions. Unlike the abbot, they were simple uneducated men. One of them even asked us what language we spoke in Australia and what was our national costume? Such naïvite frequently came up on our journey. Today television and the internet has brought the world much closer.

Everything about the monastery carried a wonderfully medieval sense of community.

10

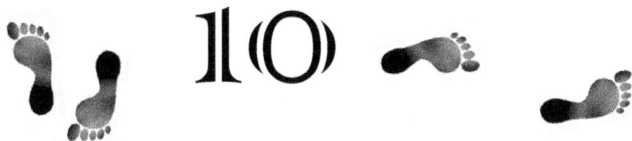

TURNED AWAY FROM ONE DOOR AND WELCOMED THROUGH ANOTHER

Do not forget the plum
Blooming
In the thicket
  Basho

Before we left next morning the abbot took us round his vegetable garden. We saw he was a natural farmer. That is where, for the first time in our lives, we saw brussel sprouts growing. None of us has forgotten the impact of the little sprouts clustered up the long stems of the plant. We had had no idea that was how they grew.

The white frost was thickly painted over logs and grass, as if an artist had been at work in the night.

We had to rub the chill of the frost off our fingers; but that was a good sign, we were told, for the day ahead. It meant a happy sunny day would follow.

As we parted from our kindly abbot he wrote down the address of another abbey we would be able to walk to in two days.

"You will certainly be able to stay the night there," he said It did not occur to him to confirm this by ringing the sisters.

We deliberately swung to the southeast. We had had a discussion over the map and saw we needed to avoid the great city of Bordeaux that was coming up; and that decision was to lead to some very interesting experiences.

A quiet and uneventful day followed in which we walked some 25 kilometers and it was getting dark as we arrived on a remote hill with one huge tree and beyond it the tall and serious nunnery we had been sent to. When John rang its bell the door immediately swung ajar, just a crack. It was almost as if someone had been watching our approach. It opened wider and an imposing nun in black stood silently there.

John explained that the abbot of Bassac had suggested we come here, that we were pilgrims on our way to Santiago and had stayed with him.

She took in his words, looking over our group, and still said nothing. I would not call the expression on her face a welcome.

When she spoke, her voice was pained. "No. You cannot stay here. This is a spiritual retreat." Then as if her first words would not be enough to convince us, she added, "Anyhow we are full; and several of our nuns are sick." We all noted the nervous strain in her voice. If this abbey was solely a spiritual retreat, why did she need to add words?

She was already closing the heavy door on our faces when John hurriedly got out one more question.

"Excuse me. Can you tell us where we will be able to find some accommodation tonight? We had expected to stay here and it is late. Will we find a cheap place in the next town?"

She paused then said quickly. "Oh yes, you will have no problem," and then the door was closed, almost into our faces. Had she answered too glibly?

We were ten kilometres from the next town and it was getting darker. With this unexpected disappointment, none of us had much energy. But there was nowhere nearby to turn to. We could only go on. It was a challenge that called on our strongest resources. Clutching at her assurance of a cheap place ahead, we directed all our energies to getting there.

By the time we got down to the highway, it had grown totally dark and was lightly drizzling. So we divided into two groups to hitchhike, making sure the girls were clearly visible in the headlights of approaching cars. As French drivers on main roads were not usually responsive to hitchhikers we hoped the sight of children would soften them.

I feared conditions were against us. It was Saturday evening when everyone would be going out to have a good time. Who would want to pick up strangers in the dark, whether they had children or not, especially now it was getting wet?

And if no-one stopped, what were we going to do? Or if only one group got a lift, what would happen to the other?

I stood at the first point with Rebecca and Emily, while John and Cassandra walked a further 50 yards down the road. Though we were showing up in their headlights, politely signalling, no cars were slowing down. We were beginning to sag.

Then a little station wagon had passed us and slackened its pace. It was stopping for John and Cassandra. The driver opened a door and they clambered in while we intently watched them. The car had not moved on yet. Then slowly it began to move. It was backing towards us, and the door opened again.

"Hop in" John called, "He's taking us all." A huge relief!

The driver was called Francoise. He was a young countryman, about nineteen. He was on his way home for the weekend from the local Agricultural College.

He said he would take us to the next town where he was also sure we would find a place; so we relaxed and chatted with him.

Francois stopped in the middle of town and made enquiries. "No, its quite wrong, there is nothing here," he told us, "only one big expensive hotel." So much for the nun's assuring words!

Francois was comforting. "Not to worry. You will have no problem finding rooms in the next town. It is a bigger place." As we drove on the initial strangeness between us disappeared, and he suddenly said "Perhaps you could sleep in our barn? "

What a wonderful thought! Lying down in soft hay. "Yes," we told him eagerly. "We would like that."

"I will make a phone call to my parents," he said and stopped by a phone box.

"I told them that you are Australians and they said you must come

and stay in our house, not in the barn" he said when he came back. "There may not be enough beds, but we have plenty of blankets." That sounded wonderful. But still I was glad we had earlier in the day picked up food supplies.

At the end of a long drive a big old farmhouse welcomed us with beaming front lights. As we pulled up, his family was waiting for us. We were introduced to the whole of the Colombeix family. There was Francois's father and mother, his seventeen-year-old sister, Anne-Marie, two cats and three large dogs.

We were hurried into a grand old kitchen where a fire was burning in a huge ancient fireplace. Three legs of ham were hanging from the rafters and a grandfather clock was ticking. We had stepped into the heart of the house.

A long dining table, already set, filled the centre of the room, with benches rather than chairs on either side.

As our packs were stowed in a corner I rather apprehensively brought out our food contributions. Mme Colombiex impatiently waved them aside. It was plain that their house was bursting with its own produce.

As we sat down, Anne-Marie, as if this was their regular nightly procedure, wheeled the television to the head of the table and switched it on. It did not seem to matter that it was in the middle of a programme since no-one paid it any attention but left it quietly talking in the background. Later when we had finished eating, in the middle of another show it was just as abruptly switched off.

Dinner was served. Mme Colombeix and her daughter dished out a traditional evening soup of fine-chopped ham and cabbage and grated carrots, with pieces of bread soaked into it. In earlier times such a soup would have been the evening meal for farmers, dinner having been eaten in the middle of the day.

The second course was a puree of fish and potato. Then Francois lifted down from the rafters one of the great hams I had been admiring. It was cut into thick slices and fried with haricot beans. Finally we had a platter of local cheeses, a bowl of walnuts, bunches of grapes and a plateful of honeycomb from one of their hives. The meal was a cornucopia.

The big farm dogs under the table were on the watch for food scraps and our children delighted in their company.

Talk moved to their property. "We have a family tree going back to the fifteenth century. My family has been living in this house from that time." There was no son, and so Mme Colombeix had inherited it.

The place was a treasure from the past, even down to the hand-woven linen sheets we would find on our beds.

The major crop of the farm was grapes, which were sent to town to one of the cognac factories. The property was two hundred hectares, big for France, but once it had been a thousand hectares. Then gradually it had been shared out amongst generations of sons. When Francois graduated from agricultural college he would join his father in running the property.

M. Colombiex took John into the cellar at the start of each new course to ritually choose a fitting wine. John had never seen an impressive collection, as he looked around with ignorance at the vast collection of bottles.

The family was very interested to hear from us about Australia, but showed no interest in our pilgrimage.

They rarely had visitors and told us eagerly of a time when French-Canadian relations had come over to France and stayed with them. Remembering Francois's uncertainty about bringing us home, I saw how privileged we were to be here.

By the end of the meal I was giddily swimming in wine and could hardly keep my eyes open, especially through the additional strain of French conversation. Our children were even sleepier. As my French grew incoherent and our girls drooped low, Mme Colombeix saw it was time to make up our beds.

She told us in passing, "We have forty bedrooms in the house." So why had Francois wondered if there would be enough space for us? She answered this unspoken question when she added, "but we have closed most of them off."

Before we were taken upstairs, Anne-Marie led the girls and me through the garden to the lavatory. It was a small building a walk away from the house. Its one room contained a long low timber settle built against one wall that consisted in a row of openings into the darkness below. Here, the family could sit companionably together and discuss the tasks ahead.

In a house with forty bedrooms and its first television set, no modern lavatory had been included. This family still lived in the style of their ancestors.

When we were shown to our beds, Emily was given a cot. A surprise for her. I guessed that as she was small for her age, they thought she was younger than ten. So, to her amusement she was given the privilege of sleeping in the ancestral cot. It turned out she could fit in it easily as it was very long with high timber sides, more like a child's narrow bed.

Next morning we were up early, eager to explore the farm. It had free-ranging turkeys, ducks and hens. Only rabbits were kept in cages. Looking more closely, we were shocked to see the rabbits' weeping eyes. They had myxomatosis. The French consider they still make healthy food for the table.

Back in the kitchen, the girls were amused by Francois throwing grapes into the air to be caught by his high-jumping dog.

Mme Colombeix asked us, "Will you stay and join our Sunday midday dinner? Francois will take you to the next station later." We were delighted.

"While I am preparing the dinner, Francois and Anne-Marie will take you for a drive around our district. My brother-in-law has asked you to have aperitifs with his family."

We had a lively morning. Both Francois and Anne-Marie were

enjoying our visit, and all their reserve had gone. They took us to see a fine local dolmen called *Pierre-Follie* and we told them about the others we had seen; then to a ruined tower and to their old local church. At the end of the morning we called at their uncle's house to share in the strong French tradition of aperitifs. He was the local mayor and his wife their mother's sister.

Then back home to a bountiful Sunday baked dinner.

Afterwards, replete and totally satisfied, we were dropped off by Francois at their nearest railway station, a sleepy little spot, to get the train to Perigeux. This was a substantial city where we knew we would find accommodation to sleep off the pleasures of the last few days.

After he had left we learned we would have to wait four hours for the train, as this was Sunday

Cassandra pulled out the inevitable pack of cards and we started another family game of zilch.

"Do you remember in Scotland how we were tipped out of a café for doing this?" Rebecca said. "The café owner was really shocked to see you playing cards with us kids. He said it was the devil's work."

The train made up for its tardiness by speeding all the way to Perigeux. We stared out of the carriage windows, soothed by the train's rhythm and the knowledge that we had now come almost halfway to Santiago.

Perigeux was an even bigger city than Chartres. We were given rooms in a rather depressing run-down seminary. "Cities will never be for us," we said with conviction.

101

CRO-MAGNON MAN

What a splendid day!
No-one in all
The village
Doing anything
   Shiki

When we woke, we were eager hurry out of Perigeux on another local train into the countryside.

"What about stopping here for lunch?" Rebecca suggested when our train came into a small valley enclosed by low hills.

As we unpacked our picnic we were joined by an over-friendly inquisitive beagle.

"Where has he come from?" Emily wondered. "There are no houses round here."

"Well, he looks too well-bred to have come far from home."

We were delighted to have him join us, though we were careful not to give him any scraps. After a short while he wandered on.

"It'd be great to take a dog on a pilgrimage," Rebecca said. "I wonder if anyone ever has?"

"Pilgrims have gone on horse-back and someone once took a donkey to carry his bags," I said.

"Imagine having a donkey and a dog along? Wouldn't that be fun?"

We saw on the map that Les Eyzies was not far ahead, so we decided to stop there for the night. We had come into the Dordogne region and were passing through beautiful countryside, a wooded region with a broad flowing river. There were old broken-down windmills on the hills, once used to grind the wheat for bread.

At this point we stepped into an adventure.

Cassandra: *We stopped for a while to pick miniature wild figs.*

We wandered on and as we turned the corner we saw ahead of us halfway up a cliff a collection of tiny white-washed houses and a notice saying there were famous caves here. That caught our interest immediately.

We were directed up a wooden staircase to a hut for entry tickets. We were the only visitors.

The guide led us down a low wet tunnel cut through rock into a chamber. From here the floor of the cave had been excavated so we could walk through not hitting our heads and with the unfolding beauty at waist height. There were none of the stalactites and stalagmites we were expecting but the walls and ceiling and floor were covered with the most extraordinary forms of crystal, very beautiful. They had expanded into flowers and a variety of fantastic shapes, even tiny crosses, all protected from onlookers by wire mesh.

This amused Emily. "Those crystals are like animals in a cage. They are pushing against the mesh trying to get out," she said.

We got so enthusiastic pointing out the wonders to each other that the guide was concerned.

"Don't touch the crystals! They will break," he warned us; but we would never have done that.

Our guide impressed us when he told us that Cro-Magnon people had lived in this valley, though this cave would have been too small for them.

Fifty years ago a local archaeologist saw water seeping through the rock halfway up the cliff. He started digging. It was a personal quest that took three years before he discovered the entry. With the ruthless ignorance of those times he cut the sunken pathway through the rock and chopped out any crystals in the way so he could set up this small tourist attraction.

It was here in this valley that the first Cro-Magnon skull had been discovered. Neanderthal man had also lived hereabouts as the famous Lascaux caves were not far north.

Cassandra's words, written that night, capture what this adventure meant for all of us.

The whole valley gave me a thick feeling because so much had happened here. We felt privileged to be the only visitors that day and were full of wonder at it all.

The Cro-Magnon world had been 18,000 years ago, in the late Ice Ages. At that time the climate was unimaginably harsh, winters lasting nine months of the year.

Continuing beside the river, we came to an enormous statue of a Cro-Magnon man. These people were shorter than us but very powerfully built. They lived on the edge of forests and hunted in groups, creeping very silently close to kill their prey, their only weapon a stone-headed spear.

We were full of thoughts as we walked into Les Eyzies, but once there, we quickly became practical.

We sought out the local curé with our introductory letter and

found him unlike any of the priests we had met before. He was a smartly-dressed worldly old man with no interest in Father Robert's letter or in us. He was comfortably ensconced in a wealthy area, and clearly we did not fit.

There was a hint of relish in his voice as he told us, "You will not find anywhere here tonight. All the local hotels have closed now the holiday season is over."

"Then where can we go?" John pressed him. He simply shrugged his shoulders and turned away.

At the shopping centre we hurried to buy food before the shops closed. Night was falling and the air was growing chilly, though nothing like as frozen as our ancient ancestors could have been.

In *The Little Ice-Age* Brian Fagan wrote: *On the coldest days, there would be little sign of humans except for a thin tendril of white wood smoke rising from the foot of a cliff on the southern side of the valley. Even hunters would stay home through the bitter depths of Ice Age winters. The long-tusked mammoths might have been seen standing motionless, their long hair resting on the snow, their breath appearing to freeze on the still air.*

At the patisserie I asked the baker if he could suggest anywhere to stay. As he handed me a long baguette he shook his head. He warned us that the situation was worse than the priest had suggested.

"You won't find anywhere tonight. There is a one-day strike on today through the whole of France. Every hotel, bar and restaurant in the country is closed."

We were shaken, and it was rapidly getting colder.

The woman standing in the line behind us heard this. She had a suggestion. "Check out the camping resort. They have a few rooms they regularly rent out. You may find one still empty. Ask the tourist bureau if they are."

It sounded like a slim chance but we grabbed it, thanking her gratefully before we hurried out the door.

"Yes!" the woman at the tourist office told us. "We have two

empty rooms on a nearby farm. I will give them a ring." Our relief
was enormous, for none of us favoured the prospect of sleeping on
the road in the cold or struggling on to another place. And there was
nowhere else to turn for the whole of France was in the grip of the
same strike.

The farmer and his wife came to the door together when we arrived.
The tourist office had rung. They were so eager to have us, they both
wanted to show it to us as we were their very first guests. They were
thrilled when we said how we appreciated their new building.

It was a cabin with two well-furnished bedrooms, a bathroom
and a kitchen.

"This furniture came from my mother's house," the woman told
us." She died two years ago. As this cabin was empty, we decided to
rent it out." The rooms were furnished with her lovely solid glowing
old pieces of furniture. They warmed our hearts. We immediately
booked the place for two nights.

When we were on our own, I said, "We can sleep in tomorrow.
We won't be going anywhere."

John added, "And to hell with that unctuous priest."

We were starting to comfortably spread through the rooms,
when John had a further thought.

"I have just added up how far we have walked. It's two hundred
and four kilometres. That's quite apart from train trips and hitch-
hikes. So now we are seasoned pilgrims. Let's celebrate by eating
out tomorrow in an elegant restaurant."

When we woke next morning, the sky was a pale pure blue, like
the virgin's cloak, the mountain air crisp and cold. Holiday time!

We washed our travel-stained garments in the bath. Some of
them had been walking with us for two weeks as we had only been
able to wash our lighter clothes as we went. Now we could work on
our heavy garments like jeans.

As there were no laundrettes in country France at that time
we made up a long clothes-line in the garden by joining together

lengths of string. Everything dried quickly in the crisp sunshine while we lolled around and read.

That evening we took time to dress up in style, or as smartly as our small stock of clothes and large stock of ingenuity allowed us. There was even a long mirror to parade in front of.

It was not difficult to choose an elegant restaurant. There was only one. But it turned out to be all that we desired.

The French eat late at night so we were the first to arrive; but already the tables were arranged with gleaming rows of glasses and settings of solid heavy elegant old style cutlery. The girls were impressed.

"I've got three wine glasses and a water glass," Rebecca said. "We all have. How much do they expect us to drink?"

On other occasions when the girls had eaten out with us in France it had always been in simple places, so now they took in the wonder of this experience, absorbing every detail.

Though elegant it had a naturalness that immediately put us at ease. This is usual in good French restaurants. Even on rare occasions when John and I had eaten in Michelin-starred restaurants, the friendly courtesy of the waiters enriched our experience.

On this evening, we pored over the menu for a while before we chose which of the four fixed price menus we would share between us.

It was normal at that time to do this when you took children to French restaurants, for the French did not have child size servings.

The tables near us were filling. "Look at that little dog over there," Emily whispered. "They've let it into the restaurant."

A smart Frenchwoman at the next table was dining on her own, except for the company of her small fluffy dog sitting quietly at her feet. She had a dish of meatballs and vegetables in front of her and was adding mayonnaise and salad to it and stirring it together. We saw her put the bowl down on the floor in front of her dog and watched fascinated as it began to eat. Who was she, a local countess perhaps, that she could get away with this? Or was this really acceptable in smart French restaurants?

When our first course arrived our attention became concentrated on our own table. We had four bowls of fine-shredded vegetable soup; that was easy to share.

The main course turned out to be more challenging as we all wanted to have some of each of the four delicious dishes. We had ordered two servings of a delicate local trout baked in butter with crisp almond flakes scattered over them, one of roast duck and one of rabbit, with salad accompanying them.

Our meal was a blending of elegance, fine cooking and country naturalness. When the cheese trolley was wheeled up with all its fine local cheeses, John and I hovered. The girls were more interested in the sweet trolley that followed, each sweet dazzlingly elegant.

At the end of the evening, full fed and soaked in the elegance of our surroundings, we sang as we walked home through the chill night under a sky crowded with frosty brilliant stars.

It was strange to think that those same stars would have shone on Cro-Magnon and Neanderthal people infinitely long ago.

12

WHAT ABOUT THE ORPHELINES?

We had wonderful two nights in the convent where I had
my own room with its own tiny sink and view over the garden.
  Emily

On the next leg of our walk we actually rambled down the wrong road, the only time on our pilgrimage. We did it by simply straying from one sentier path to another. It was easy to do because they were so close to each other. "Finalement," as the French would say, "pas sérieuse".

The path we wandered onto seduced us. It was so beautiful. It wound through oak and chestnut forests with the sun shining through brilliant leaves and a constant drift of older yellow and brown leaves adding to the thick padded carpet we were stepping on. Our two days in Les Eyzere had been so relaxed that we were in no hurry.

Our feeling is expressed in this photograph of Rebecca, absorbed in her book as she walked.

Yet this turned out to be another of our longest walks, another

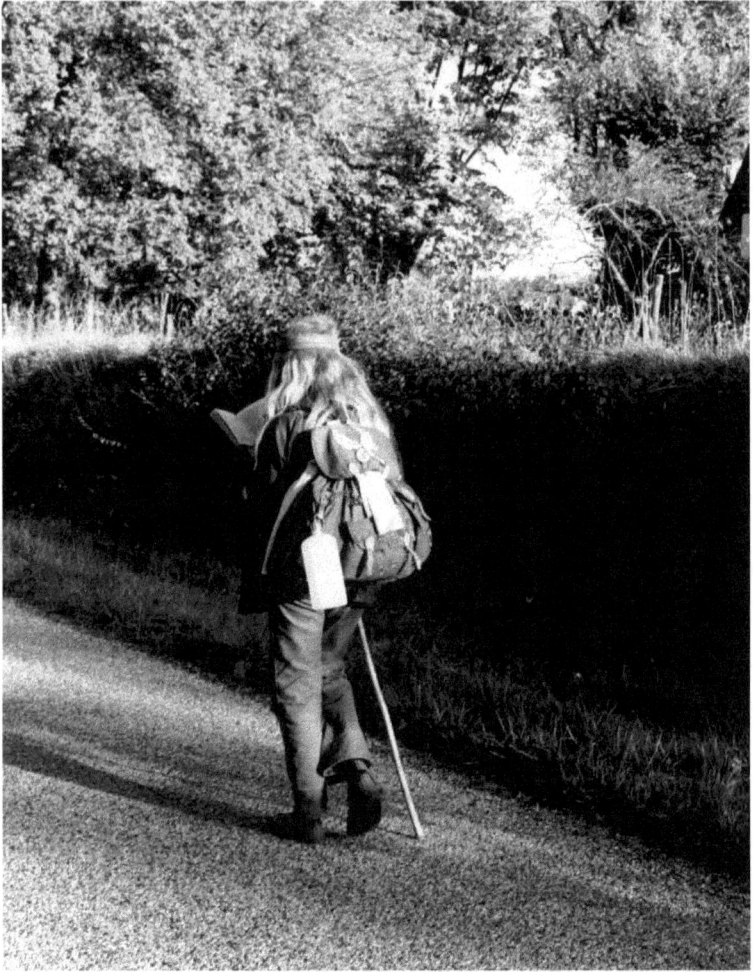

huge thirty kilometres, because we wanted to get to Sarlat for the
night. John knew it was a beautiful medieval protected city and
felt we would have no problem in finding accommodation. That
pushed us on. In spite of the distance we found ourselves there by
mid afternoon.

We spoke to a local priest and he knew exactly where to take
us. He drove us to the very top of a steep hill above the city to a
convent where the nuns ran an orphanage. He had heard they had
recently started taking paying guests who had a connection to the
Church. He was sure they would welcome us. And they did.

The convent had wide sweeping grounds and wonderful views over the countryside.

"I hope we can play with the orphans," Emily said and the others agreed eagerly. They had missed out on meeting any children at the school at Airvault, and they wanted company.

One of their favourite books had been *The Little Orphelines*. It was set in an orphanage in Paris and, rather like the famous Madeleine stories, was full of their adventures. These books gave them a highly romantic view of the liberal and joyous life in French orphanages.

But the girls never got a chance to learn about orphans as we did not see them here either.

Our accommodation stood on its own. The Visitors' House was an old building the nuns had just restored so recently that we would be their first paying guests, eagerly welcomed.

Several nuns showed us through it, vying for the pleasure. For they had all had a hand in planning and putting it together; it was their child, each room prettily furnished. We were delighted with it and immediately booked in for the following two nights.

The nuns were a bright-minded, well-educated, interesting group. I don't know how the members of different convents are selected, but for us these women had a special quality. We wanted to keep hanging out with them.

We were served an elegant evening meal as we had at Airvault, and in this case, the nun who was serving us stayed on, talking with us while we ate. She was very interested to hear about our experiences on the Way.

Next morning John, who always has had a super-abundance of energy, woke up with an absorbing project for the day. He was going to take the measurements of the beautiful Romanesque chapel in the grounds and compare its geomettric proportions to others he had collected.

One of the nuns obligingly hunted out a tape measure and he

was already at work when the girls and I set off on a different exploration.

The Dordogne River was below us, wide and quick flowing and clean. We scooped up the water in our hands, and found it sharply cold. No chance of dipping our feet in here, but we floated sticks and watched as they swung and eddied downstream.

And this turned into a leisurely day of play for us all.

13

AND HERE COMES SPAIN

Our childhood was a series of adventures, never predictable
but always interesting. It was one of recurring movement
and unreliable destinations, cocooned within a solid family framework
that gave us a home wherever we were.
   Emily

John was still carrying the copy of *Le Monde* he had bought at Periguex station. We had hardly opened it. So today on our second day of rest at Sarlat, we took turns reading aloud the world news. Not easily done in French in that densely intellectual newspaper.

That was when we learned that the war in the Middle East was actually ending on this day.

"Who won?" I asked.

"It's not clear. They say it is a cease-fire. I think other countries helped negotiate that."

It had not been as quick as the previous Six Day war between these people, but looking back on it now, I see how it led to a drastic change in relationships between the countries involved.

Afterwards Egypt moved away from its long close relationship with Russia, a friendship that threatened the western allies, and Syria became Egypt's closest Arab ally. And most important of all, the US began its present commitment to Israel.

All that still lay in the future. At that time we were simply glad to learn that peace had returned.

When we left the nuns, we did not go back to the beautiful city of Sarlat, though we had intended to. It was too far below us, and our path lay in the opposite direction.

Bergerac, the next big town on our way, was one of the post restante addresses we had set for our family and friends. We felt rather starved for letters, so we sped our pace by hitch-hiking. We were having a spell of doing that.

Again we divided into two groups. My three were picked up immediately by a young policeman. He had a day off work and was on his way to Bergerac to parachute. He disapproved of our hitchhiking, but still generously took us with him in his tiny Renault.

We expected to get there well ahead of the others, but they had been picked up immediately after us by a young woman in a faster car. So they were already coming out of the post office as we turned up. We saw by their sombre faces that we had no mail.

"Why hasn't anyone written to us?" said Emily petulantly, "We gave them our addresses and we've been writing to them."

We were deeply disappointed.

At that moment it felt a long time since we had left Australia. This adventure was demanding so we were having a wave of homesickness, a longing to share our life with others. We could hardly believe there was not one letter to soften our loneliness.

After taking another supply of money out of the bank we pondered. It was clear that everyone's spirits needed reviving. By now we had been on the road for fifteen days, and it had often been demanding, even with our lovely breaks. The map showed a monotonously flat uninteresting land ahead.

Then John had an inspiration.

"I have just worked out that we are only three hundred miles from the Spanish border. We could catch a train today and be there tonight. Wouldn't that be amazing?"

Of course we jumped at that suggestion. There even was a train we could catch this afternoon.

"What is Spain like?" Cassandra asked, knowing we had spent three weeks travelling through it in our early twenties.

"It was old-fashioned in the 1950's," I said. "Far behind the rest of Europe. It was like stepping back into history. And the people were deeply, seriously Catholic. Not like the French or Italians."

Old Spain was divided into huge estates where the serfs lived on boiled grasses and roots and the better off survived on lentils, black sugarless coffee and bread, while many children died of hunger. Education was in the hands of the Church and they deliberately kept most of the population illiterate.

In 1931 the Republican Party was elected to change this. They were opposed by the nobility and the church, and quickly the military was encouraged to revolt. Thus was begun the Civil War. The great democracies refused to help the elected government while Fascist Germany and Italy sent their forces to aid Franco.

A passionate movement of outrage swept idealists from around the world to form brigades, reflected in Ernest Hemingway's *For Whom the Bell Tolls* and Arthur Koestler's *The Yogi and the Commissar.* In the end, General Franco won and controlled the country for the next forty years until he died some two years after our pilgrimage. How were we going to find Spain today?

The train was going to take several hours. When we had settled in, Cassandra suggested to the others, "I know what. Let's play Heads, Bodies and Tails?"

Emily bounced at the suggestion.

"I'll get the paper and pencils," Rebecca said. "I've got some at the bottom of my pack."

Each girl faced away from the others so they could not see what she was drawing. Firstly it had to be a head, at the top of a long strip of paper. A head of what? Anything they liked, but preferably something bizarre. Maybe an amusing person or some strange creature, or just anything they fancied. They folded over the paper, leaving only the neck visible, and passed on their paper to the girl

beside them. Next they concentrated on drawing a body.

This game had been taught them by their grandfather, Jimmy. As an artist he set high standards when they played. They could always rely on him to draw funny fantastical parts. The game filled the journey with joy and fun. At the start there were not many in our carriage, but by the time we pulled into Bordeaux it was different.

The doors were flung open by an impatient crowd who came pouring in, their arms full of big awkward bundles. In a moment they had taken over every spare seat. Their loud talk and heavy garlic-laden breath filled the air. It was exciting.

It took us a few minutes to work out they were speaking Spanish and probably a dialect. They were grape-pickers on their way home at the end of a season's work, dark-skinned and smaller than Frenchmen, the older men smaller than Cassandra or Rebecca. The carriage now vibrated with their chatter and stayed that way.

The train pulled up decisively at the Spanish border. Being a French train, it was not going any further.

Chaos broke out. Everyone and their baggage wanted to be first. With a babble of excited voices, they pushed into the aisles, careless of everyone else.

Before the European Union was formed, crossing a national border was a big process, for each country was an island in itself.

Passports and visas were carefully examined outside the border before you were allowed to cross. This time I was impressed by how quickly and efficiently we were all moved through. That was probably because so few of us were foreigners.

We hurried after the crowd to the next train.

"Check where it is going, " I called to John. "It mightn't be ours."

"It's all right," John assured me; he was always more relaxed on these occasions. "There is only one train leaving. It stops at San Sebastian and goes on to Madrid. Everyone will be catching it." Still we hustled our children along because we could see the locals were competitively crowding on board and we did not want to be left behind.

John and I were going to have to rely on our scant store of Italian to support us in Spain, as we had done last time. On a simple level the two languages had a lot in common.

We got seats but did not dare relax. San Sebastian would only be a short distance off.

"Get ready," we warned the girls, "they mightn't give us much time to get out." And that proved true. The train pulled up, we dropped onto the platform and a moment later it was hurrying into the night.

Such a contrast! San Sebastian was quiet and tranquil: moonlit with golden street-lights. We put on our packs and the girls grasped their staves.

It would be a long walk to the youth hostel, for the map showed it in a park on the far side of town. But we were glad of exercise after sitting in the train for so long.

When we got to the hostel, the front door was locked. Our hearts pounded. But as lights were still on in a further room we knocked loudly and the warden let us in.

John booked us in while the girls and I crept ahead to the women's dormitory. The lights were out so we had to grope in the dark for empty bunks. Fortunately there were several close to the door. The lights must have been out for a while because the room was filled with the quiet breathing of sleepers.

We never met our night companions, either then or in the morning. When we crept out at our usual early time they were still motionless bundles under their blankets. It was a pity not to have met some of them. We would have to discover Spain for ourselves.

14

SATURDAY NIGHT IN ORIO

Wake butterfly -
It's late, we've miles
To go together
     Basho

"For our first Spanish breakfast, we ought to have their traditional one," John said as we walked into town. "I remember it from our last time here. They make a wonderful thick hot chocolate drink with churros."

"What's a churros?"

"You'll see."

We had to visit several cafes to find one that had it on the menu. Then we found one with a waiter in a long white apron who was serving it. The traditional Spanish breakfast consisted of hearty white mugs of rich thick black chocolate and saucers of sugared churros. These were sticks of batter, thickly sprinkled with sugar. They were crunchy!

Our girls were delighted with them, but privately on this second tasting, John and I felt let down by our memory. The churros were too sweet.

After this indulgence we asked the waiter far a path going westward along the coast. Being limited by our scant vocabulary and small pocket dictionary, he was not able to help us.

So we turned once more to John's natural sense of direction. That led us to a beach of fine white sand, the famous Bay of Biscay. This sea has long been known as dangerous, wild and tempestuous.

But to day it was different. The bay was shaped like a capital C lolling on its back and the sea was a beautiful sparkling blue as though summer had just returned. The balmy air was warm and a salt breeze was blowing. It was Heaven!

We took off our sandals and rolled up our pants and started wading through the water's edge with the lovely sandy beach rising to our left. We weren't the only ones using the beach as a passage.

Dozens were walking to the city with their trousers and skirts tucked up, some ploughing through a foot of water.

"Adios!" a Spanish woman greeted us as she passed, her dress hitched high.

The next paddler was going the other way. He did not see us, as he was holding the morning newspaper in front of him and reading. His assured bare feet probably took this journey every day.

After him came the most bizarre sight of all, a smart young businesswoman wading to work, her shoes in one hand and a briefcase under her arm. She smiled and called a greeting to us as we passed.

"Spain is going to be fun," Cassandra said.

At the far end of the beach we climbed a hill, leaving San Sebastian far below and taking us exactly where we had been hoping, along a narrow country road running west.

Though we did not know it, we had come into the Basque region of Spain, a big area of the northwest. There was a smaller Basque region just over the border in the southwest corner of France.

The Basques are an ancient people who managed to keep themselves separate from the rest of Europe for over five thousand years. They were in this region long before the Gauls and Iberians arrived.

Today they have a population of two and a half million, the bulk of it in Spain, and still have their own distinct language and culture. They have even managed to survive Franco's pointed hostility. Our pilgrimage would continue to take us through their territory, though their separateness was not obvious. We only learned of their culture through talk.

We weren't the only ones walking along our road. We would soon find walking was the natural form of travel in Spain as cars were more rare here than in France. Several people were strolling ahead of us and others passed us the other way.

Up here we found groves of pine trees, small apple orchards and farms with haystacks neatly built around poles. We stood on

the crest of the hill admiring them. This was the children's first real taste of Spain. We were relishing the sea below us on one side and blue hills on the other.

Then we became aware of a jarring sight. Below us was a great half–constructed expressway. Change had abruptly thrust itself into the countryside, bringing a speedier world with it.

At the end of the afternoon our path brought us to the little fishing port of Orio. Not long ago it would have been an infant village, but now it was a leggy teenager. Like the expressway, it was pushing old-style buildings aside to make space for bigger and more modern ones.

The dock had not changed. There were brightly painted blue and red and green fishing trawlers in the harbour. Groups of women knelt on the pavement, mending the fishing nets spread out in the sun.

We walked into town to find beds for the night. It was hard making our way up the crowded street carrying packs, for we had arrived at the 'paseo', the traditional Spanish hour for social strolling, especially on a Saturday night.

Also, the local men had been at sea all week, and turned each Saturday night into a celebration. The town tumbled with energy.

Charcoal braziers on the pavement outside the smarter restaurants had already been lit. We sniffed the scented smoke appreciatively. Big fresh fish from the trawlers would soon be grilled on them.

We did not have to walk far before we came across an old hotel that looked promisingly modest. It offered us one big basic L-shaped room with beds for us all. The girls gratefully kicked off their shoes, chose their beds and relaxed.

"See you later," they said as John and I went off. We were looking forward to exploring this little town without packs, having a first taste of Spain on our own after a long time. We were going to hunt out a modest restaurant.

"Let's have a sherry," John said, another traditional taste of Spain. The bar was small and crowded and full of life. Along the counter saucers of tempting little tapas were set out. We shared a Basque dish called a piperade. It was made of green capsicums, tomatoes, garlic, ham and eggs. It was not an omelette, nor exactly scrambled eggs, but something deliciously in between, and a little larger than a snack. Tapas can be quite simple, such as a morsel of

seafood cooked on the grill or a dish of shining black olives, or they can move into more sophisticated little dishes. At that time they were rare in our lives.

In fact, we had not eaten tapas since we were last in Spain in the 1950s when a Spanish friend had taken us out in Madrid. As we moved from one bar to another he told us it was the custom to spend hours wandering with your friends between smart *tavernas* all evening, until at midnight you ended up in a restaurant and paid serious attention to a dinner. At that time, he said, some of the best *tavernas* in Madrid offered as many as forty or fifty tapas to choose from.

Our bar this evening was modest but delightful. The noise was so loud we could hardly hear each other but we didn't need to speak; we were busy absorbing our surroundings. Fishermen were gathered around us, and gangs of labourers working on the expressway had come for a drink of sherry after work. We had to pull ourselves away, to start looking for a restaurant.

Down a flight of stairs in a narrow side street we found it. One look inside that plain cement building showed us what we had been looking for, a fisherman's haunt. We hurried back to collect the girls from the hotel.

"It's really close," I told them, "but so hidden we were really lucky to find it."

The low-ceilinged semi-basement room, like a ship's galley, was crammed with long tables covered with red-checked cloths. We were taken to the only one unoccupied.

Service was brisk. The young waitress asked our order then roughly put down a carafe of dark red wine and a plate of thick-cut heavy bread and was gone.

At the next table a group of cheerful exuberant young men were singing at the tops of their voices, laughing and shouting, for Spaniards loved to sing and shout at the top of their voices.

No one paid any attention to us. In southern Italy we would have been stared at. But there was a natural courteous reserve and good manners here that is unknown in Naples.

Cassandra laughed at their private rowdiness. "No wonder their families send them out to sea," she said.

At the other tables the seamen were not as young. They were less loud. Sitting on their own were two definitely older men, short and nuggetty, weather beaten and assured. They were leisurely rounding off their meal with cognac and cigars. Were they the captains of the little boats tied up to the pier?

Except for the waitresses there were no other women as in the bar. It seemed Spain was like southern Italy in that their men went out together on their own, even when they had been away all week.

We talked freely, feeling certain that none of them understood English and also aware we were wrapped in a gauze of others' noise.

Our first Spanish meal was tasty and different. Firstly we were brought a big silver tureen of thick soup. As I lifted the lid we breathed in a heavy perfume of garlic and many vegetables. I ladled out helpings into bowls and handed them round.

The second course was one huge freshly caught fish grilled with oil and garlic on the charcoal brazier. It came surrounded by a mass of crisp chips and another carafe of local wine for John and me; and finally slices of ice-cream cake.

Walking back, we passed smarter restaurants where customers sat at small tables and were quiet and refined. But there was none of the zesty atmosphere we had shared in. We were so glad of the choice we had made.

15

MARIA'S WASHING MACHINE

There were times of longing as the grape-pickers
called us to join their merry crew, and hunger
as we learned that shops dont open until eleven
    Emily

When we emerged from our plain hotel next morning, we found a changed Orio. Sundays in Spain brought out its serious side. All the shops and restaurants were closed, and the town silent, except for the clear ringing of the church bells.

"Where will we go for breakfast?" Cassandra said cheerfully, not expecting a problem; however, nothing seemed to be open anywhere.

After much grumbling of empty bellies we found there was only one baker's shop open in town. The gratified and tantalizing smell of hot fresh bread was drawing a crowd to the door. We queued with the others.

When it was our turn I held out a handful of coins and pointed to a large local loaf. Despite the scent, the choice of bread was limited compared with France.

Still, tearing chunks off the hot loaf was delicious. It made up for the lack of butter and spreads. But this would be all we would have this morning except for water from a nearby tap.

We left town, guided by two teenage girls who had also been in the queue. With a few semi-Spanish words and the usual sign language, we had asked directions and found we were going the same way.

They were planning to spend the morning watching a local football match on the beach in the next fishing town. We were glad we had caught their attention, as everyone else had vanished indoors with their bread.

The girls were not in a hurry so we slowed down to fit their casual pace. After we parted, we passed through much the same countryside all afternoon.

At one time we looked down on a field a long way below us. Four men were hard at work, even on Sunday. They had slashed the

grass and were raking it into piles, then throwing it onto the wagon, while the carthorse dozed lazily in the sunshine.

The road took us through Guetaria, a tiny sleepy fishing port. As we passed a church the congregation, smartly dressed, was just coming out. We could not help staring. The children held our attention. They were dressed all in white or in red, a dazzling effect. There were also others with tartan kilts or tartan trousers, and one man had a tartan shirt. What was the meaning of this Scottish burst in faraway Spain?

One family carried this even further. Their large family of children, both the boys and the girls, were wearing a particular clan pattern. With no way to speak to them, we could only remain mystified.

We passed out of the small town, as easily as we had come in. Beyond it, cliffs reached high above us and blue sea broke onto rocks below. We wanted to get off this road as noisy Sunday traffic passed uncomfortably close, and it was hot. We decided to look out for a beach.

We found one at Zamaya, where we bravely paddled in rather chilly water. A few others were bolder and were actually swimming.

It was a lovely little beach, neglected and old-fashioned. All we required to complete our happiness was some food. We were hungry and it was time for a picnic. Surely by this hour shops would be open?

We found the local bar open, and we hurried in.

The shop was stocked with spirits and wine, but the shelves had no food at all. There were no dry biscuits or olives or even packets of nuts, none of the snacks we would have found in France. We could hardly believe this, so kept on looking further through the shop and still being disappointed.

All we could have for lunch were the last scraps of our cheese and salami, finishing off once again with tap water. Needing to move into a better-stocked region, we found a local train was going to a big town in an hour. Though it was a long wait it seemed worthwhile to get us out of here. We had no idea how far we would be taken, for we had not yet bought a local map.

Wanting to buy tickets, we discovered that they were sold only at the very last minute, just before the train pulled in. As if to keep you on your toes with anticipation!

We sat for a while on an empty platform. Gradually others came trickling along.

At last with a shrill triumphant whistle, the train pulled in.

It was an old train, with hard uncomfortable wooden slats for seats and an amazing old-style cowcatcher in front of the engine.

After such a long wait we were surprised to be taken on a very short journey at a ponderously slow pace.

There was a group of young men in our carriage singing loudly and unselfconsciously at the tops of their voices. Travelling third class is a great way to share local life.

Lunch was our first thought when we arrived. We had no problem finding it in this big modern town. We sat looking down on the boats in the port, happily munching.

We decided not to stop overnight. We would prefer a town that was less modern. Someone told us we would find what we wanted at Montrico. It was not much of a walk and was also by the sea, a comfortable old town with cobbled streets. Already throngs of smartly clad people were out for their traditional stroll, a big crowd this time as it was Sunday.

John and I remembered watching these formal parades in the 1950's. How they had changed! At that time young girls walked together demurely and self-consciously, or, more boldly they leaned out seductively from flower-bedecked balconies above our heads.

Groups of young men could only eye them from a distance. Discreetly further off, the parents chatted with their friends whilst supervising. The scene was much more casual today. But still the parents kept their eyes on their children and still main square was dominated by the energy of the church.

We had hoped to get assistance from the local priest as we had in France; but today we could not get near him. We would have to look around for ourselves. But after a few enquiries we discovered that we had come to a town where the rooms were too dear for us.

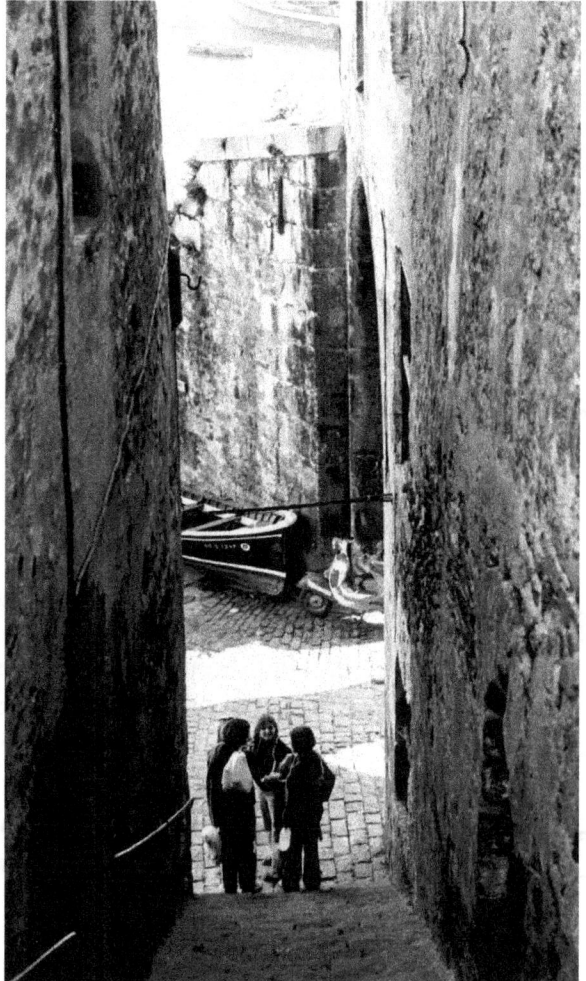

John stopped an elderly black-clad woman and asked her advice. She surprised him by immediately replying in French.

Taking in our rather run-down appearance, she took us away from the centre, down a neglected unlit back lane. She explained that a woman let out bedrooms here. The place did not look appealing from the outside but with no other choice we knocked on the door.

No one came when we rang the bell, so we sat down and waited.

"Of course there's no one at home," Cassandra said. "She will be out walking like everybody else. Let's look for a restaurant?" But there were none nearby.

A local cinema was about to show Ben Hur. A crowd of shouting youngsters clambered at the doors. They were not concerned with the paseo.

Everyone else in this town was enjoying themselves. Why were we spending our days looking for meals and beds?

At this introspective moment a small neat woman came up, taking out her key. Maria Cortez was home. We were very glad, even a little desperate, to see our predicament may have ended.

"Yes I have rooms for you," she said immediately. Her price was higher than we had paid so far but we accepted that. To economize, we chose a single big room for us all with two double beds and a thick mattress on the floor. Once we were inside, we found the house was clean and pleasant and comfortable, a contrast to the lane outside where people peed against the wall.

Having dropped our packs on the beds we went off to find dinner, following Maria's directions to a bar selling tapas.

We stayed with her for two nights, and we quickly grew fond of Maria and her home. We wondered if her warm excitable temperament was typical of Basque people. After all she reminded John and me of our Basque friend of the past, Jesus Matteo.

We guessed Maria was comfortably off, for she owned two apartments linked by a hall. This made a roomy establishment.

Now that her family had grown up and gone she had many empty rooms to rent out. We saw she was glad of our company.

In the morning I asked her if we could wash some clothes in her laundry. She agreed with alacrity. It must have been obvious to her how dusty and travel-stained we had become by now.

Perhaps we did not deserve to have been so fussy about our choice of a lodging? She took us to her laundry where one glance at our vain attempts to scrub the stains off our clothes led to her becoming quickly involved.

"Mal mal!", she said, shaking her head at the grime.

"I have a washing machine," she told us. With an owner's pride in her voice, she pointed it out to explain what she was saying.

Then she added generously. "We will use it." I picked up from the
pride in her voice that in Montrico a private washing machine was
a treasure.

Doing the washing together turned into an exciting multi-
language process and made us friends. She piled in our clothes and
set the machine whirring in the midst of a flood of women's talk.
She was teaching us new words.

Maria much admired our daughters' long thick hair, especially
Rebecca's blondeness. She was further drawn to Emily as the
obviously youngest member of the family. Rebecca being as tall as
Cassandra, and often looking older than her, the gap between her
and Emily looked larger than it was.

"Em-il-y," Maria said lovingly, lingering over the separate syllables
of her foreign name. Balinese villagers had done just the same. After
all, the names Cassandra and Rebecca were harder to say.

Emily was embarrassed and responded shyly like a doubtful
uncertain puppy. But she was delighted with the pair of brown
corduroy pants Signora passed on to her from her grandson.

The washing finished, Maria took us outside to her clothesline.
We passed through a room full of small cages of imprisoned rabbits
and not much else. We were unhappy to see they were being fattened
up for the table.

In her back garden we hung out our clothes on her line beside a
neatly laid out vegetable garden.

Beyond her back fence disorder reappeared. The lane was strewn
with broken glass. This came from a little factory where smashing
bottles seemed to be a regular part of their business. We worked out
that this was a very small apple cider factory.

A donkey was standing patiently while apple mash was shovelled
into his cart. His job was to carry it away. Trucks were still rare in
this traditional world.

Once we had our clothes fluttering in the breeze we were free for
the day. "Let's go to the beach," we said.

The public square was a mess when we stepped out of the front door. The litter from the night before was all around us. Yet on a bin nearby there was a notice clear enough to foreign eyes, stating in Spanish, "Keep Montrico Clean."

This time we intended to buy picnic food first. We were not going to be caught again. We were discovering that Spanish restaurants and shops never opened till mid morning and that the main meal of the day came around midday. At six or so came tapas and not before ten at night the evening meal. In cities it came later, and we remembered how in Madrid we had struggled to stay awake till midnight for the evening meal.

By now the shops had opened so we bought picnic food, then wandered down to a little beach, after stepping carefully over the fishermen's' nets on the cobble-stones. The nets were a pretty sight, every shade of blue. We had come onto a working beach.

It was too chilly for a swim so we poked around rock pools and went exploring and had a lot of fun. Later we spread out our luxurious Spanish lunch on the rocks. We had local green olives, smoked cheese and bread, a green capsicum, mandarins and even a tin of palm hearts, a new experience. A bar of chocolate and sour fizzy drinks were extra treats. That day everything tasted delicious and very foreign.

16

REMEMBERING GUERNICA

In a sorrowful voice
A cricket is heard singing
Beneath the withering grass
   Basho

We were sorry to leave Maria the following morning, but our pilgrimage called us. We gratefully packed the sweet–smelling clothes she had laundered, not knowing when they would be washed so well again, and were sorry to leave a new-found friend.

From Montrico we passed along the coast with waves below us crashing on the rocks. We sniffed the resinous pine forests and even found eucalypts growing here. How had they wandered so far from home? We tore their leaves apart and sniffed their pungent scent.

Tonight we expected to reach Guernica. For the girls that was just the name of another town to be called on; but for us the name tore at our hearts. The name had been a rallying call of the Spanish Republic during the Civil War, and a clear issue in our parent's minds.

Over lunch on the beach we told them the story. On a market day in April 1937 the centre of the town was thick with stalls, and shoppers, horses and carts. Suddenly Nazi German planes in league with Franco swooped on the market to strafe and bomb. They kept circling to chase the running people, and even the shepherds and their sheep.

The attack continued for three hours till the whole wooden town was aflame. An English journalist, who was almost mown down himself, publicized this first assault deliberately targeting civilians. The armaments factory had not been touched.

The outrage galvanised Picasso to create this anguished painting of the horror; but the conservative world remained oblivious and aloof. The Republic was shattered. It was a prelude to the World War that followed only a few months later.

With some foreboding we made our way to Guernica, and found that all the wooden buildings were gone, replaced by modern concrete and plaster. It was dull and not a little forbidding.

Feeling uncomfortabe, we took a bus through the outskirts of town to a big cheap hotel built after the bombing, yet so old-fashioned it even had a copper plug in the bathroom. We were the only diners in the echoing old dining room. They served the traditional dinner we had come to expect, a thick Spanish soup and rough local bread, and a bottle of local red wine for John and me.

It had been an uneventful day. My diary was a blank. "Do you realize we walked twenty five kilometres today?" Cassandra said. It was now so easy for all of us, young Emily as well, for we had all grown strong and resilient.

17

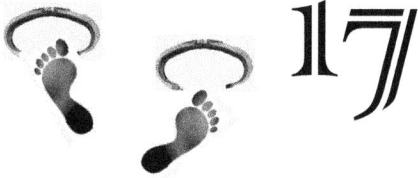

ALL SAINTS DAY

This book is so evocative and in the moment, which was after all the way we travelled. We had no internet or phone so we were much more in the present and at the mercy of whatever befell us. It did make us enjoy the fabulous experiences more, since we had not known they were coming nor did we plan ahead for them as people do today.
   Rebecca

We woke fresh, ready for new adventures. We had discovered that Guernica's market was on today so we were there early. It turned out to be different from any market we had been to. On every stall there were wreaths for sale, and nothing much else. We drifted round admiring them all and sniffing the fragrant air. But why were there so many, and where were the food stalls?

Then we remembered. Of course tomorrow was the first of November, All Saints Day. The local people would be putting the wreaths in the graveyard and remembering the terrible story of the bombing. It would be a very deep occasion. After all, the first bombs had been dropped right here in this market place.

As Franco was still ruling Spain, the only safe way for the Basque people to express their long anger and unfinished grief was through putting out wreaths.

As I was wandering soberly by, I heard Emily saying cheerfully.

"Which of these wreaths would you like on your grave, Becky?"

"Come and I'll show you." Rebecca answered, equally lightly, and led her off.

Meanwhile Cassandra was telling John, "They do have some food here. Look over there." So we were able to stock up on salami and pate and fruit and home made bread. We bundled all of this into our packs and set off for Bilbao.

We were seeking a friend of our past, Jesus Matteo Garcia. (The J is a soft guttural sound coming from the back of the throat.) We had travelled with him twenty years before and remembered he had the Bilbao agency for a very elegant German car.

A kindly woman in an office helped us trace him. He was out of town just now, on a visit to Madrid; so we left a message to say we would be back.

We met Jesus on an empty highway. We had been standing for

a long time waiting for a lift, and saying impatiently, "Is there no traffic in this country?"

Finally, we saw a fast elegant car coming down the road. In a second it had passed us. Just as quickly it started reversing. A door was flung open and we were invited in by a delightful and handsome smiling black haired man in his thirties.

"To Madrid?" he asked. "I will take you." Just like that! He spoke a little English. Meanwhile he drove on, fast, giving himself sustenance by swigging from a bottle of strong black coffee. He was not really in a hurry. That was just the way he lived.

It was a long lift, and by the time we arrived in the city he had planned to share his week in Madrid with us. This was our first taste of natural Basque hospitality. Maria's had been our second. For the next week he took us out each day, and even included us in a grand air display held for General Franco. We felt a little shabby alongside all the others dressed smartly in white.

From the start of our friendship he had advised us not to talk politics in Spain. As a Basque he knew discretion. We found that the only people who spoke freely were the poor. Their hostility for the government poured out of them, and they had been so thoroughly defeated no one cared what they said.

Though Bilbao was the capital city of the Basques, we were surprised to find it a dirty shabby city. Spain seemed contradictory in many ways. The people dressed with fastidious neatness in impeccably bright new clothes whilst their streets were often dirty and neglected, with old papers blowing in the wind.

Not finding Jesus in town, we caught a train out of the suburbs to get away from the slovenliness, but alas, shabbiness insistently followed us.

The local river that ran beside the railway line was heavily polluted! We had never seen anything like it; for the factories regularly discharged their chemical filth into it. This made the air in the train so foul that we hastily shut every window in our carriage.

As the train was following the course of the river upstream towards its source, we gradually left the stench behind and moved into clean countryside. Soon the river's water was fresh and tumbling and sparklingly clean. It was a sobering thought to have experienced what this clear water was innocently heading into.

We were glad to leave the train and start climbing into purple hills, like the Scottish highlands. "Enough of cities!" we said as we went on our way to Mercadillo, a very different smaller town.

Here we were in the midst of two-storey stone houses with massive stone lintels over their windows and doors. Long strings of tempting red peppers dangled down the walls, as they dried in the sun. Here we easily found a pension for the night, and after another nourishing homemade meal we had a long cosy night, one that we would be grateful for the next day.

18

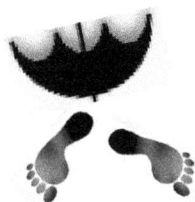

WE HAD BECOME EXPLORERS

The walk fell into an easy flow, a rhythm of simple tasks that fitted around the ever-changing countryside. We walked slowly, sometimes talking, singing, running, pausing or in silence but always walking. Some days were long when there was no bed and we had to keep walking into the falling dusk or the rain, and we had to push ourselves beyond tiredness till we finally found that extra reserve that appears just when you think you can go no further. It was a great training for later life!
Cassandra

The morning did not begin well. Our smart walking pace was interrupted when the strap of Emily's sandal broke for the second time. Though our feet were toughened by now, our sandals weren't. Cassandra had become our skilled leather-worker, repairing them unless we were fortunate enough to come across a village boot-maker. On this occasion we took off our packs and relaxed on the roadside, while Cassandra skilfully stitched Emily's straps together with a darning needle and coarse thread.

"I am not really enthusiastic about this," Cassandra said to Emily laconically. "It's breaking too often."

"Sorry," said Emily. "But I can't help it, you know. It's getting tired." Our family sandal mender was vitally important to us all. None of us could have done as good a job.

"There it is," Cassandra cut off the thread. "I just hope it lasts."

It was good she fixed it well, for we were about to stumble into an adventure where its strength would be essential.

Later in the day a sign pointed down a side-road. It simply said one word, 'Cueve'. We guessed that meant cave, for we had spotted it marked on our map. We followed its direction excitedly.

A narrow road took us to a hamlet of medieval simplicity. On the ground floor of each little house there was a cow byre so that in winter the animals' body warmth would naturally heat the family sleeping above.

There was a line of working donkeys tied up and a woman

nearby. We said *cueve* to her and she pointed to one of the houses.

The guide came out when we knocked. He was a man in his fifties. When he spoke I realised he was partially dumb and worse, what he could say was in dialect, and thus hard to talk to. His voice had a strangely dead tone and his sounds were hardly intelligible. In spite of this we managed to understand each other, but slowly and as from a distance.

In response to our question *cueve?*, he simply uttered *tarde*, and that seemed to close the conversation for him. He believed this was definitely too late in the day.

We had not expected a refusal for we had pictured the cave trip as a short interesting excursion through a cave or two; with hopefully a few traces of ancient cave paintings thrown in. Afterwards we intended to continue our walk; but this was not to be.

Seeing we were not moving off, the guide thought longer. We guessed he had changed his mind when he went inside and brought out two old pressure lamps. Putting on his coat, he gestured us to follow him. Delighted, we said no more but followed down a steep path between hedges.

The cave proved to be impressively large. Our guide paused outside and lit a cigarette while we waited in silence. Now that we were successful we were awed. We were standing on the home territory of Early Man.

The guide went to a spring and filled the paraffin lamps with water and lit them. Then he unlocked a gate and led us in, pointing to a place in the corner where we could hide our packs. He made it clear that they would not be safe if they were not tucked out of sight of intruders. It seemed that casual visitors picnicked here, for their names were burned on the walls. "A dictionary of fools" my father used to describe such sacrilege.

Once we started downhill we left such ordinariness behind. For the next two hours we slowly and cautiously followed our guide along wet difficult tracks, going deeper and deeper into the bowels of the earth. As one great cave led into another I realised there would be no cave pictures on these dripping walls.

Emily: *The guide grunted with excitement and shone his lamp around the caves. It reminded me of reading in Tom Sawyer the description of Becky Thatcher and Tom when they were lost in the caves. They were huge and awesome.*

The guide's strange guttural expressive noises came out whenever he wanted to catch our attention, like when he lifted his lamp high to show us the ceilings and the wonderfully shaped stalactites and stalagmites. I felt uncomfortable with him and very distant as we stood together in this eerie magnificent place that he obviously loved so dearly.

John walked at the back carrying the second lamp. He and I

were keeping careful eyes on the girls. We had asked them not to talk to each other so they could concentrate. We knew we could trust their sense of balance and their skill in climbing. Cassandra, knowing her sandals could be slippery, took them off at the start. She found it easier to walk barefoot on the muddy floor.

The path was so narrow we had to focus. We were grateful for the support of the hand-carved stair cut into the rock and occasional railings. It felt a strangely weird, unlikely place to have strayed into, yet exciting.

We looked up to the ceilings and stretching dimly above us saw there were stalagmites. Their changing variety and grandeur filled us with awe. Cassandra's drawing describes it well.

Emily: *The ground was slippery and crystalized into a milky colour with a pink colour every now and then. We pitied the tourists who came here in high-heeled shoes. We guessed the guide only took people here once or twice a year because he was so excited to be back here.*

One time we squeezed through a forest of petrified columns. Many ages ago the stalactites and stalagmites had joined to form a dense jungle, their rough surfaces coated with shining gleaming white crystals of limestone.

Cassandra: *I was hoping for a painted cave, instead it was wild, dangerous and awe-inspiring. We were climbing into a secret and hidden world within the belly of the earth. It was thrilling!*

On either side of the track we saw sudden drops into remote caverns thirty feet below. On one occasion our guide gathered us all around and lowered his lamp far below and moved it round. With a quick expressive hand across his throat, he almost gloatingly made it plain that a fall here would be our end.

Emily: *It was like the one I imagined Alice in Wonderland had fallen down.*

After a huge timeless time we circled back to the distant mouth of the cave entrance. I felt relieved when its silhouette came into view.

It is hard to describe the shock of change we felt as we left the cave and our silent guide and were once more on our own, walking normally down the main road.

By now it was evening and getting dark, and we had a town to get to. Fortunately it was nearby. On the outskirts we noticed a large formal Jesuit school, so we hurried in. We had no thought of looking further. We felt in need of a refuge.

John handed our letter of introduction to a priest at the door and he took it away. While waiting we talked to a beautiful dark-eyed young Spanish woman who had a group of merry children milling around her. Ruefully she told us that these five children were all hers, and the eldest had only just turned seven.

She also reminded us that as this was All Saints' Day the school was in the midst of celebrations. Still disoriented from our adventure, we had quite lost thought of which day it was.

At this point the priest came back with a companion. They had read our letter and were impressed.

"So all of you are pilgrims," one of them said in English. As they looked at our eager faces and scruffy wear, we glowed. At the same time I was feeling we had passed some sort of Rubicon and had become explorers rather than pilgrims.

"This is a Jesuit school. Today we are very busy as we have visitors sharing in our celebration of All Saints Day. But I will help you find lodging for the night. It would not be easy for you on your own since this is a holiday."

So he went off with John. Meanwhile the other priest kept us company. I was aware we were a rough travel-stained group to be welcomed so well, but he ignored this.

"It is wonderful to meet Australians from the other end of the world, making this pilgrimage as a family." He knew we were not Catholic, and even not particularly religious, but that made no difference to his benevolence.

When John and the priest came back they had managed to find us two empty rooms.

"But first you will join us for dinner," the priest told us. We were incredibly grateful after our big exhausting day.

Four of the older high-school boys took us in to dinner, a special privilege for them. They were chosen because they were able to speak with us, having studied English. This whole occasion was our first contact with Spanish Jesuit priests and their congregations. The eagerness and intelligence showed how alive and self-assured Catholicism was in Spain.

The boys escorted us into a spacious dining room with dark

panelling round the walls and they served us our meal. The first sip of that soup was deliciously sustaining, sending a shot of new energy through me. It was followed by a plate of sizzling fried eggs and bacon and, finally, a bowl of fruit. I have never appreciated a meal more thoroughly.

John was eating at a different table where he was talking with a very cultured and intelligent priest on history and politics, and the possible origin of the Basque people. He was a teacher at the seminary and a Basque, as were most of children in their school. Then he expanded the subject, going into the history of the Basque people, proud of his heritage.

Their language is different to any other in Europe, excepting perhaps Hungarian. But curiously, there may be a connection with the opposite side of the globe in Japan where many place names reflect Basque words.

The girls and I were seated with two women, also chosen because they spoke English. They told us they were here for the day's festivities. Above all, they wanted to hear about our cave experience. That suited us well. We vied with each other in re-living it as it was at the forefront of our minds.

Emily: *They told us that people mostly only went down those caves with ropes and pick-axes and often someone had been killed. We saw for certain then that there were never high-heeled girls amongst them.*

So our guide had not been dramatic, and certainly it had been no normal sightseeing trip we had insisted on. We now learned that a lot of climbers using ropes ventured much deeper than we had and that slipping on wet rocks was common. After heavy rains, water could suddenly flood up from below, catching climbers by surprise and drowning them.

I was glad we were in a safe place when we heard this. Yet when I looked at our children's eager faces, so absorbed in the telling, I felt hugely grateful for our adventure.

19

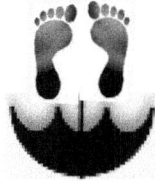

MILK CAME ON DONKEYS

A bee
Staggers
Out of the peony
    Basho

Next morning we made an expedition to a shoe shop to buy a pair of very much-needed sneakers for Emily. She was thrilled, for new clothes did not come often at that time. Cassandra probably felt the same since her mending skills would no longer be called for.

Walking through the outskirts of Mercadillo, we saw sprightly little donkeys pulling small carts coming the other way. They were bringing the milk supply and were stopping regularly to sell it to the women coming out of their houses with cans and jugs to be filled.

This is how milk was delivered in my childhood, though our carts were horse-drawn. If we needed cream for a special occasion we children walked a mile through the local bush with a jug to fetch it directly from the dairy.

Our bread too was delivered by horse and cart, and my mother often sent me out with a bucket and trowel to collect the consequent manure for our vegetable garden. I found that embarrassing and wished I did not have to do it, but I did not protest.

The Spanish donkeys seemed a charming alternative to our horses, as Emily drew them.

"Let's get one of our own in Australia," said Emily.

At that moment something bright and red fell from a cart. We shouted, but the noise of its progress over the cobbles hid our voices.

A man on a motorbike coming the other way heard us. He swung around and picked up the umbrella and brought it to us. We explained who were the owners and he kindly went after them.

When we got to Laredo we found it was a sophisticated seaside holiday resort.

It was big enough for John to lose his sense of direction.

He stopped a man and asked the way out of town. "Come," was his simple answer as he packed us into his car.

We must have shown our uncertainty when he put us down on an empty beach, so through signs and a word or two he explained why we were there. In a little while a boat would turn up and ferry us to the other side of the water.

"But there is no wharf?" Making marks on the sand with a stick, he explained that by going this way we would save ourselves twelve kilometres of walking. We were so glad to learn that.

Seashells were thick on the beach. The girls, vying with each other, made collections, listening to their soft murmurs when they held them to their ears.

"Let's each choose one for Compostela?" Cassandra suggested. "Our own scallop shell."

Meanwhile John had started building a sandcastle and was deeply absorbed in tunnelling below it. He could never leave sand alone. Soon we all joined him.

After we had picnicked, we were glad to lie down on the sand for a siesta. We were still tired after our cave adventure.

Some time later our boat turned up. The boatman, to our surprise, turned out to be a young boy of eleven or twelve. But he was practical, even professional, collecting a small fare before helping us on board. Despite the choppy water, it only took a few minutes to cross to the other side.

We were walking off when a loud voice called out peremptorily. A smartly uniformed member of the Civil Guard came up to us.

Until that moment, I had not noticed we were passing a gaol. Now I fully took in the forbidding structure. There was no mistaking it. The man was the guard outside.

In a voice of hard authority he addressed John and me in Spanish. "Who are you? What are you doing here?" we gathered he was saying.

Suddenly we felt threatened. What did he want from us? We could be stepping into a delicate situation. Our lack of Spanish would be no help here.

With careful politeness we brought out a phrase or two, supported with gestures. "Australians." we said, pointing to our group, "tourists walking," pointing to our packs.

"Oh turistica," he said, relaxing, and for the first time he smiled, "Au-stria," he added, with an emphasis on the first syllable.

It seemed we were approved if we were Austrians for he gave another smile and waved us on. Now it was our turn to relax. He had just enjoyed asserting a little power in a boringly monotonous job. We had brought some colour into his day.

Though ready to accept Austrian nationality, we still felt shaken by the experience. Until we had this encounter we had been resting comfortably in our status as tourists.

The experience was a reminder of what it must be like for Spaniards who opposed Franco's dictatorship. We shuddered for those held behind those heavy walls.

In the late afternoon Emily again said, "I'm tired." That was understandable.

John thought of a distraction. "Could you give me a hand working out where we are going?" he asked her. "You will need to check on our map. I'll help you to start with."

We soon discovered that she had a greater grasp of map reading than we had expected. She competently followed the relationship between the map and the landscape and got us back on our way. That distraction revived her and helped us all put the mood of the gaol behind.

Between the quiet road we were on and the beaches we were passing, there was a scattering of pretty little white holiday cabins and low stone walls, then green fields and an expanse of mountain ranges. We had come to a village called Noja.

I said, "Let's see if we can stay here to-night."

But we had come to a tourist resort. As always, sophistication and high prices were hand in hand.

We walked along the water's edge till we came to a hotel. Perhaps this would be a cheap one? No such luck. The manager was no more drawn to us roughly dressed travellers than we were to him. His prices were far beyond the reach of pilgrims.

"How unfriendly tourism makes people," we agreed loftily as we walked off, thus managing to keep our confidence in place as he had just told us that we would find no cheap in this area.

But after a while we came to a simple low-built hotel that stood separate from the beach resorts. We were actually welcomed in. It had the plain style we had become familiar with in Spain.

For dinner I spent some of my birthday money I had been holding for a special occasion. This gave us a great meal of a wonderful fish soup followed by tortillas and then crème caramels. The comfortable beds were also a better standard than we were used to, with pretty cotton bedcovers and reading lamps. We even had a deep bath and then relaxed to read in bed with the sound of the sea beyond.

20

EVERY END HAS ANOTHER BEGINNING

In later years we looked back and were proud at how far we had walked. The Camino was not generally known then. I looked forward to getting to Santiago and was sad we did not make it, but by then we were on to our next adventure.
   Emily

The next day we walked along the low green hills behind the seaside, until catching a local train into Santander. We were full of anticipation as this was where money and letters should be waiting. We got to the post office at seven at night and found it was still open! But again we were disappointed; there were no letters.

So we walked onto the bank. And there, abruptly, our whole happy world came tumbling down.

At the bank John comfortably reached into his pack for his passport and found nothing. Unconvinced, he searched more thoroughly. Then together we went through both packs. My passport and the girls' were in my pack, but his was missing. When had we seen it last?

"We had them all at the Spanish border," I said. It must have been after that."

John remembered, "After we crossed the border I used my passport to draw our last lot of money out of the bank. I must have left it with the teller when I changed francs into pesetas."

The Santander teller promised to ring the bank at San Sebastian, but as it was Saturday, we would have to wait until Monday.

Then, using my passport, when we checked to see if our money had come through as planned, we were told, "No money has come through." It sounded impersonal, but was the truth.

We were shocked and very surprised! We were expecting it from various reliable sources and there had been enough time for it to arrive. There was the regular rent from our house in Sydney sent by the estate agent, and money from John's firm through our accountant. We were also expecting cash from Philip, a friend in London who had bought our old car, Organ Morgan. The Spanish banking system was not particularly slow and, as we were to discover, it had just not been sent.

The message was clear: This was the end of our journey. It is one thing to go boldly adventuring, and another when the world crumbles down. We felt lonely and abandoned.

Today, when twe are so closely connected through internet and mobile phones, it is hard to understand how isolated people could become. At a time we needed public telephone boxes to ring anybody, and international calls could be a nightmare. We could not even ring our English friend, as we did not have his phone number. To make it worse it was Saturday night and everything was closing.

We only had a bit more than a hundred pounds. What should we do?

We decided to wait in Santander till Monday morning to give our money a last chance of coming through.

By devious means we found a big room in a pension in the centre of town, ensconced within a private house.

We had little sleep that night.

As we talked tensely, we could hear outside the walls the loud wild celebrations of a Saturday night that went on till two in the morning. We woke with a strange weighty feeling.

After breakfast John rang Jimmy.

"We are leaving for Australia tomorrow evening," he told him. "But I will leave money for you here to tide you over till yours comes through," he added; and so he saved us.

On one hand it was our muddle that we thought he was leaving later, but on the other the fates had intervened. The loss of John's passport meant we had rung Jimmy in time; a day later and he would have already set out for the other side of the world.

We had enough to get to Positano, and were sure the other moneys would follow in time. We had to remind our shaky selves that none of it was lost, just delayed.

It was sad that our pilgrimage had come to an end, but also strangely acceptable. We certainly had travelled a long way and the girls had managed magnificently and, like others before us, we could complete it another time. Life flows on and the joy was in the doing rather than the accomplishment.

We were restored by talking to Jimmy, and felt aglow to be going to Positano. The

original plan had been that when we had finished our walk we would mind his house over the coming winter. We were still to do this, but a little earlier.

We arranged that if the passport could be traced, then John and Becky would hitchhike to Chartres and pick up the baggage we had left with Dominique, and catch trains to Positano, while we others would go there more directly, taking a train through the Riviera.

We filled in our weekend in Santander by setting out on another walk to a little Romanesque hermitage outside the town. It was on a hill with trees behind and a field in front. A local man unlocked the door for us.

This simple dignified building dated back to the first years of the crusades. It had a pitched roof and a plain belfry. The hermit had worshipped here alone. Our visit felt like a last gift, linking us to all the spiritual seekers who had ever paused here.

On Monday we confirmed the safety of John's passport. The teller had discovered too late that John had left it and had expected him to come back shortly. When John had not turned up it was passed on to the head bank at Bilbao. That was conveniently near, and we would go there and collect it.

We were a quiet group when we set off this morning. Becky for the first time for years felt sick and had slept badly and Cassandra had a splitting headache. We had waited to see if any mail came for us this morning; but again there was none. John hitchhiking ahead on his own to make sure the passport had got there, and we more slowly. We had to wait nearly an hour for a lift as we were four and plus all our packs.

We came into the city past the great busy port with its crowd of shipping, a wide river of dull-coloured water and rain. A crane was swinging cars across the river onto a waiting ferry.

We found the British Embassy just as John came out. He waved his passport triumphantly. And with him was Jesus, after a gap of twenty years! He had matured from those heady days and his thick

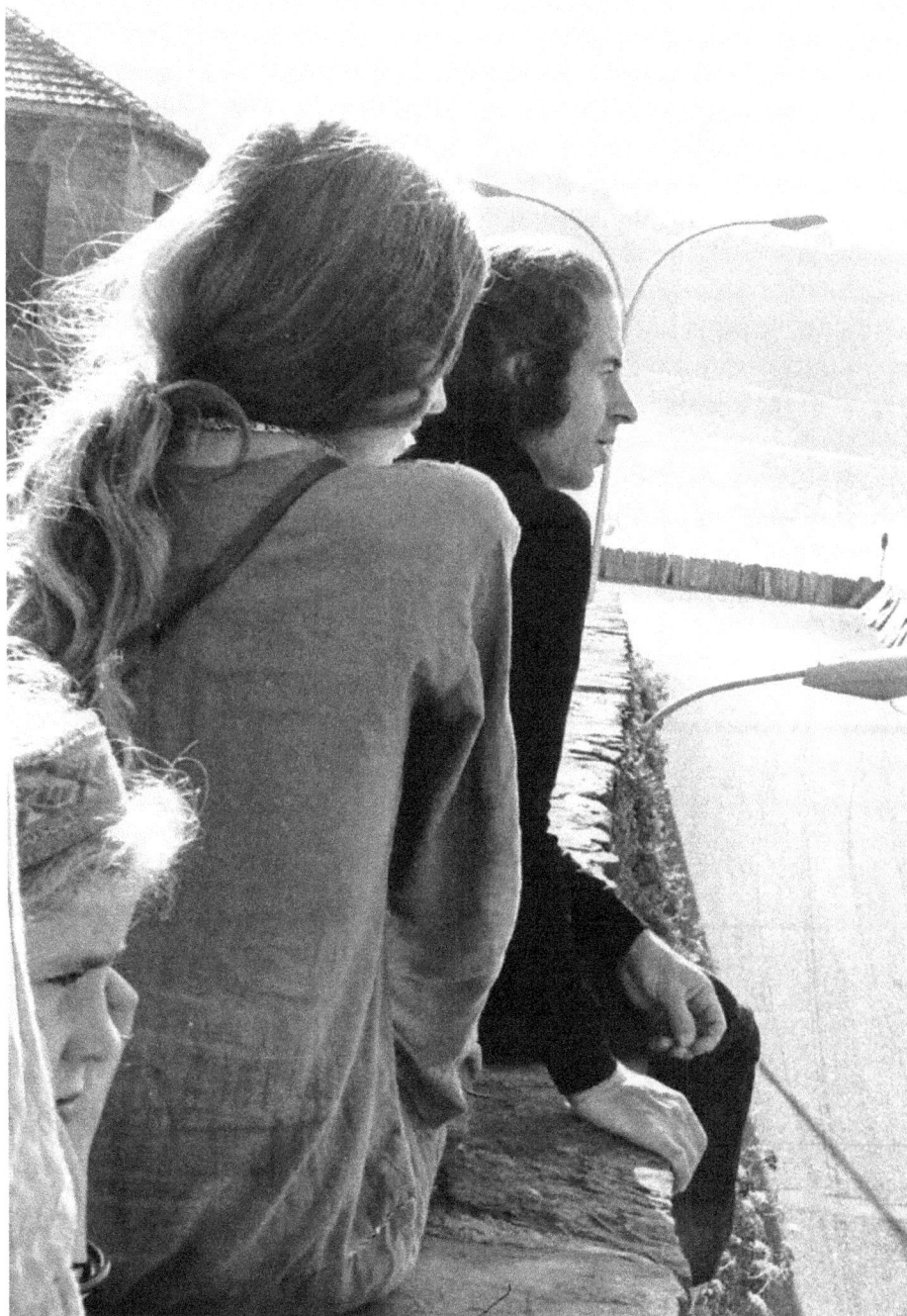

black hair was now snow white. But he had the same charm and elegance and love of life. He was still a fiery dynamo.

I remembered his high spirits on our first drive together. Whenever he saw by its number plate that we were passing a Bilbao car, he would toot madly; a greeting to a fellow Basque.

He took us to lunch, a great feast of Basque delicacies, course after course of squid cooked in its own juice and pig-trotters in a sauce, and I have forgotten what more.

After taking us to meet his wife in their flat, he drove us out of town to a two hundred year old cottage they owned where we could stay the night and rest until the next day when we would set off on our two ways to Positano.

Looking over our pilgrimage now I see it was our growing resilience over those weeks that carried us over the humps so we never lost our optimism or our vision. We are all of us still resilient, yet I realise we did not do this on our own for we had the unanticipated support of nearly everybody we met. They made our eager rather innocent journey flower. The memory of it remains in these pages.

The Statistics of our Pilgrimage

411 kilometres walked during 22 walking days, and average of over 19 K/d. Our children were just 10, just 14 and 12 and a half.

Note that the names of Basque towns have been changed over the years.

Date	Route	walk	hitchhike	train, bus	walking da
9 October (Tuesday)	Chartres to Saumur			241	
10 October (Wednesday)	Saumur to Fontevraud.	16			1
11 October (Thursday)	Fontevraud to Thouars.	22	13		1
12 October (Friday)	Thouars to Airvault	24	2		1
13 October (Saturday)	Airvault to Aulnay.	8	8	100	1
14 October (Sunday)	Aulnay to St Jean-d'Angelay	19			1
15 October (Monday)	St Jean to Saintes	30	3		1
16 October (Tuesday)	Saintes				
17 October (Wednesday)	Saintes				
18 October (Thursday)	Saintes to Bassac	15	7	26	1
19 October (Friday)	Bassac to La Coronne	26			1
20 October (Saturday)	La Coronne to Brossac	30	32		1
21 October (Sunday)	Brossac to Perigeux		24	109	
22 October (Monday)	Perigeux to Les Eyzieres	14		34	1
23 October (Tuesday)	Les Eyszieres locality	14			1
24 October (Wednesday)	Les Eyszieres to Sarlat	30	8		1
25 October (Thursday)	Sarlat to Montford return	8			1
26 October (Friday)	Sarlat to Bergerac to Spain	5	89	300	1
27 October (Saturday)	San Sebastian to Orio.	22		21	1
28 October (Sunday)	Orio to Montrico	20			1
29 October (Monday)	rest				
30 October (Tuesday).	Lequeito to Guernica.	25		21	1
31 October (Wednesday)	Guenica to Bilbao to Mercadillo	11		59	1
1 November (Thursday)	Mercadillo to Castro Urdides	26			1
2 November [Friday]	Castro Urdides to Noja	26	21		1
3 November (Saturday)	Noja to Santander	12			1
4 November [Sunday]	Santander locality	8	7		1
5 November (Monday)	Santander to Bilbao		95	10	
6 November (Tuesday)	Bilbao	hitch and train to Positano			
	totals in kilometers	411	309	921	22

21

IN RETROSPECT

No sooner had the spring mist begun to rise over the field
than I wanted to be on the road again.
The gods seem to have possessed my soul
and turned it inside out, and
roadside images seemed to invite me from every corner..
Basho

People have wondered what sort of lives our daughters lived after their unusual childhood. Here is a brief summary they have shared with me.

In 1974 our family returned to Australia and our daughters went to school after years of home schooling. Cassandra and Rebecca went to a country high school, and Emily to a one-teacher primary school with only a dozen students. The routine and rules were hard to adjust to for a while, but the girls were not held back by any schooling they had missed. In fact they were often ahead.

Emily said recently, "I don't see what I missed out on."

At times they did feel starved of new books as we could only carry a few with us on our travels (English books were not yet available in Europe). Yet they also had the luxury of endless free time to read many times over the few precious ones we had, and to write their own short creative stories.

For Emily what was lacking over those years was not having enough other children to play with. This changed when we moved to Scotland for three months so the girls could attend Kilquanity House - a wonderful alternative school in Scotland based on the famous Summerhill that focused on creativity, fun, self-government and adventure. As it was small, only thirty-five kids, they were a close crowd. The experience stayed in our hearts as an essential shaping of our lives, and an invaluable balance for our girls.

After such a varied education all three girls still chose to go to university, and have since explored a variety of unusual and interesting careers.

Emily became a potter and a nurse (*EmilyLaszuk.com.au*). Rebecca taught children with disabilities and combined that with an online business (*WaterPumpsNow.com.au*). Cassandra has been an archaeologist, a DJ and entrepreneur, and now is an energy healer for professionals working with clients across Europe (*HealingTheDeep.com*).

Of the three, Cassandra has continued to travel most. Her wildest adventure was sailing across the Pacific in a yacht at twenty-two for a year with her partner. Breath-takingly beautiful yet dangerous, their trip included surviving a super typhoon with sixty foot waves.

Seeking inner stillness after ocean life, she went to live on an ashram, then co-founded and managed a healing business in Sydney, the AcuEnergetic School. Ten years ago she took this therapy to Europe where she lives between beautiful rural places in South West England and Provence. Adventurous life-changes have remained part of her natural life pattern.

Rebecca has had a long highly skilled career with small children with special needs and their parents. That has been her passion. But she has also set up two different businesses and they have each thrived. Like Emily, she has a family property and loves to be close to nature. The spaciousness of that life supports her creativity.

Emily, who had always wanted to be an artist, studied ceramics at the Sydney College of the Arts. She has run a commercial studio ever since, supporting their farm. She has also become a nurse, so has two careers going side by side. Life for her too has a close connection to the land. Each of the girls have chosen to live in more bohemian communities, as they feel at home with open minded people who accept people's differences.

Rebecca shared, "Our early years of travel led us to want our children to also go overseas while they were young for a taste of the experiences we had. Travel had opened us to compassion and strength as well as independence."

Both Cassandra and Rebecca saw how the pilgrimage linked us to the footsteps of devoted pilgrims over the centuries. There was something slow and medieval about the very act of walking for such a long time. For when you leave the fast modern world to walk the ancient paths you slow right down. It becomes a meditation on the road.

Cassandra laughed, "Now I know how to travel with an absolute minimum of belongings. It helped us refine our notion of what we thought was essential.

"The pilgrimage showed me it is possible to have an inspiring, and even radical vision and then make it happen. I found it amazing how welcoming people were to us because they saw we had a purpose that was bigger than ourselves, and they connected with the purpose. Even the private French people welcomed us into their family homes, showed us their region and helped us on further.

"I also loved the Basque people of northern Spain. They were so passionately alive. I was very aware of their fierce independence and continuing battle against Franco.

"On our pilgrimage we had unexpected adventures every day and were often hungry for spells, but in the end we were never stuck. We learned that something always turned up, and we learned adaptability."

All three girls received from their unusual childhood a deep trust in themselves, great creativity, courage to live differently and an appreciation of the whole, varied world. It was a way of life that at times asked a lot of them, and yet gave them everything in return.

www.ingramcontent.com/pod-product-compliance
Lightning Source LLC
Chambersburg PA
CBHW071758090426
42737CB00012B/1860